Renewal Coaching Workbook

PRAISE FOR THE *RENEWAL COACHING WORKBOOK*

"With this comprehensive *Renewal Coaching Workbook*, master coaches Reeves and Allison have wrapped practical tactics and interactive exercises with an overarching strategic approach to sustainable personal and organizational change. Unique in its genre, this workbook is firmly grounded on a fundamental principle—help the reader find purpose and achieve a legacy for the greater good."

—Luis A. Martinez, M.Ed., author of *Getting There: High Performance Strategies and Tactics for Career Decisions*

"The *Renewal Coaching Workbook* is a wonderful resource for individuals who are going through change, and for those helping others through difficult times. I was engrossed from the beginning. A major strength and uniqueness is the interactive nature of being able to use the workbook as well as the website. At a time when millions of people have to rethink their purpose, careers and lives, this workbook provides an important tool for their development."

—Patricia Boverie, Ph.D., author of *Transforming Work: The Five Keys to Achieving Trust, Commitment, and Passion in the Workplace*

"In addition to the seven elements of Renewal Coaching (Recognition, Reality, Reciprocity, Resilience, Resonance, Relationship, and Renewal), one could easily add 'Realization' in that this companion workbook to *Renewal Coaching* is all about making things happen! Elle Allison and Douglas Reeves have created a wonderful tool to help an individual, organizational leader, or leadership/executive coach reach sustainable personal, professional, and organizational improvement and success through a carefully constructed, research-based workbook that will result in a powerful 100-day action plan. This is not a book to passively sit back and read; it is a rigorous interactive roadmap for action."

—William L. Coale, Ph.D., CEO, Coale Education Group

"The *Renewal Coaching Workbook* is a wonderful piece of work. It is filled with important information and exercises which guide the reader to discover and live from all they can be. The book not only provides a new frame of reference through which to look at life, but the skills to do it. This excellent book will become your personal coach to call upon whenever you like. I recommend it highly."

—Brenda Shoshanna, Ph.D., author, *Fearless: 7 Principles of Peace of Mind* (Sterling Press, 2010)

"Life is a wonderful teacher when we take time for reflection. This book provides the structure most of us need to access learning and self-awareness in a thoughtful way."

—Paul Axtell, president, Contextual Program Designs, corporate and university trainer, and consultant

Renewal Coaching Workbook

Douglas B. Reeves and Elle Allison

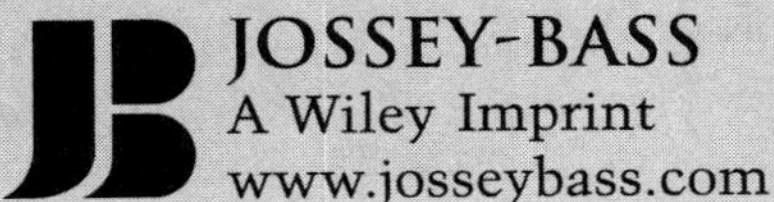

Published by Jossey-Bass
A Wiley Imprint
989 Market Street, San Francisco, CA 94103-1741—www.josseybass.com

Jossey-Bass books and products are available through most bookstores. To contact Jossey-Bass directly call our Customer Care Department within the U.S. at 800-956-7739, outside the U.S. at 317-572-3986, or fax 317-572-4002.

Jossey-Bass also publishes its books in a variety of electronic formats. Some content that appears in print may not be available in electronic books.

Library of Congress Cataloging-in-Publication Data
Reeves, Douglas B., 1953–
Renewal coaching : sustainable change for individuals and organizations / Douglas B. Reeves and Elle Allison. — 1st ed.
p. cm.
Includes bibliographical references and index.
ISBN 978-0-470-41496-5 (cloth : alk. paper) 1. Organizational change. 2. Employees—Coaching of. 3. Personal coaching. 4. Change (Psychology) I. Allison, Elle, 1960– II. Title.
HD58.8.R386 2009
658.3'124—dc22

2008050157

ISBN 978-0-470-41497-2 (Workbook)

Printed in the United States of America
FIRST EDITION

PB Printing 10 9 8 7 6 5 4 3 2 1

CONTENTS

Dedicated to the amazing and generous clients and coaches of Renewal Coaching

ABOUT THE AUTHORS

Douglas B. Reeves is cofounder and chairman of Renewal Coaching and author of more than twenty books and fifty articles on leadership and organizational effectiveness. An internationally recognized expert in leadership, Reeves was twice named to the Harvard Distinguished Authors Series and was recently named the Brock International Laureate for his pioneering research. His work appears in national journals, magazines, and newspapers and has been translated into six languages. Through his affiliations with RenewalCoaching.com and the Leadership and Learning Center, he delivers more than eighty keynote addresses annually around the globe to audiences in North and South America, Europe, Asia, and Australia.

Elle Allison is cofounder and president of Renewal Coaching and has worked with clients in health care, business, education, nonprofit organizations, and government agencies. She also founded Wisdom Out, an organization that shares the strategies used by wise people, couples, and organizations to face whatever challenges come their way (www.wisdomout.com). Since 2000 she has conducted countless interviews of people who were identified as being wise by someone who knows them. What these Wisdom Makers have to say will be published in the forthcoming books *What Wise People Do* and *What Wise Couples Do.* She is a member of the National Speakers Association and, through her affiliations with Wisdom Out and RenewalCoaching.com, reaches a diverse audience by delivering engaging and informative keynote addresses and seminars on Renewal Coaching, wisdom, and leadership.

ABOUT THIS BOOK

Since the publication of *Renewal Coaching*, the world has changed. The global economy has transformed the lives of millions of people, delaying retirements, dashing dreams, and undermining the fundamental confidence that people have had in their ability to achieve their hopes and dreams. If we have learned anything in this time of upheaval it is that ***technology, intelligence, and analysis are not enough. The world needs renewal and resilience***.

The good news is that since the publication of *Renewal Coaching*, we have heard from people in every walk of life that even in the most challenging of times, they can make a profound difference using the tools of *Renewal Coaching*. They have learned that it is both possible and necessary to bridge the gap between ideals and reality, and that *Renewal Coaching* can serve as the essential tool for transforming theory into action. Most importantly, we have accumulated quantitative and qualitative data to support the essential truth of *Renewal Coaching*. People are neither motivated nor inspired by a 4% gain in earnings, test scores, or donations, but they are resonate with a commitment to the Greater Good. Whether the economy is depressed or booming, people need a connection with meaning more than money.

Readers will approach this book from many different perspectives. If you have already read *Renewal Coaching* and you are an experienced coach, then jump into these exercises and prepare to accelerate your learning. If you have not yet read *Renewal Coaching*, then you will find it a useful prelude to the Workbook. If you have not yet visited the Web site, www.RenewalCoaching.com, then you will find the assessments a useful guide to your personal journey toward renewal. If you are new to the coaching profession, then we particularly invite you to consider Part Three of *Renewal Coaching* so that you understand both the theory and the business philosophy supporting the creation of a Renewal Coaching practice. Traditional books are a one-way exercise in communication—the authors speak and the readers listen. This book is decidedly different. The authors are listeners and learners, and we welcome enthusiastically the participation of readers—both professional coaches and new entrants to the profession—to a dialogue with us. In our next book, *The Renewal Coaching Fieldbook*, we will feature success stories of Renewal Coaches, and we actively solicit your ideas, challenges, and success stories.

We wish you a renewing journey.

—Doug and Elle

INTRODUCTION

Our book *Renewal Coaching* has already had an international impact. We have observed coaches at many levels, from those who are leaders of large organizations with thousands of employees to those who are independent practitioners. We have heard from coaches in the business, education, government, and nonprofit sectors. In the United States and abroad, their reports are consistent: we need renewal now more than ever, and we need practical tools to help us sustain our work. The *Renewal Coaching Workbook* is the answer to those requests. In these pages you will find interactive worksheets, assessments, and prompts to help you think, write, react, and most important, inspire others in your journey toward the greater good. Pick up a pen or grab your laptop; this will not be a passive piece of work. The greater your engagement and the more intensive your response to the prompts in this workbook are, the more valuable your insights will be. Sustained change is never the result of words, however inspiring and heartfelt they may be. Our research and practice, along with that of the many experts we have studied, have led us to the unequivocal conclusion that sustained change is both profoundly difficult and profoundly worthwhile.

THE CASE FOR SUSTAINED CHANGE

There is no dearth of information on strategy, planning, and execution. Academicians and practitioners have published exhaustive reviews of research and practical application on personal and organizational change. Nevertheless, we remain far better at initiating change efforts than at sustaining them. Although a few writers (Bossidy and Charan, 2002) retain enthusiasm for "the initiative" as a change mechanism, most people regard the announcement of change—particularly with the term *initiative* included—with the bemused expression of Dilbert. Far from inspiring the troops to actions, most initiatives are little more than rhetorical flourishes that represent the temporary triumph of hope over experience.

What Makes This Time Different?

When leaders announce an organization change or when individuals write a New Year's resolution, the missing essential question is, *What will make this attempt at change different from the past dozen that we have tried?* We have posed this question to many leaders, and their answers are sincere but insufficient. "This time we're going to get lots of input," they say, forgetting that surveys, focus groups, and broad-based input were used in the past as well. "This time we're going to have a strategic plan," they enthuse, forgetting that their bookshelves are creaking under the weight of three-ring binders of previous strategic plans. "This time we're going to focus on execution," they continue. The list of what makes "this time" different is long on illusion and short on substance. If the focus is on strategy, planning, and execution using the same tools and orientation of the past, then we should not be surprised that the results are the same, with nearly all change initiatives failing (Kotter, 2007).

The Price of Cynicism

What happens after years of failed New Year's resolutions to diet, exercise, visit loved ones, or get more organized? People eventually have one resolution left: to stop making New Year's resolutions. The resulting cynicism and lethargy can occur early in life. Stanford researcher Carol Dweck (2006) has demonstrated the profound and lasting effects of how children think about their abilities. When they become persuaded that talent is simply a lucky break, a gift from an unknown deity, or otherwise unfathomable, they become unwilling to work toward a goal. Work, in their view, is not the key to success, and their failure to work hard leads, not surprisingly, to failure. This confirms their negative viewpoint. Similarly, adults at every stage of life can reach alternative hypotheses that lead to hope or to cynicism. Renewal offers a perspective that encourages the eighty-six-year-old to lead a life of service and purpose long after people twenty years younger have concluded that they are too old to make a contribution to society. Cynicism, on the other hand, leads those at every stage of life into despair and hopelessness. Organizations, too, suffer from emotional debilitation, when even vital changes are greeted with apathy or resistance.

The Promise of Renewal

Fortunately, Renewal Coaching offers hope for coaches and leaders at every level and for clients in every organization. In this workbook you will find intensive assessments that call for deep reflection and complete authenticity. Because the coaching relationship is confidential, now is the time for challenge, not flattery. Whatever challenges you face—and we have observed clients with enormous organizational, physical, emotional, and personal challenges—the path toward renewal offers a journey in which the effort is great but the gains are greater. You will achieve these gains not by reading this workbook but by using it. Before you proceed, either pick up a pen or log on to www.RenewalCoaching.com and get ready for the first of the exercises that will help you along your journey.

HOW TO USE THIS WORKBOOK

The *Renewal Coaching Workbook* is designed for four possible audiences. First, independent coaches may use it to deepen their relationships with clients. The coaching profession is complex and varied, including executive coaches, life coaches, business coaches, leadership coaches, and many other variations on the theme. Renewal Coaching is not a replacement for these approaches but a framework that adds value to them. If you already have a successful coaching relationship as a client or as a coach, we encourage you to continue it and expand that relationship using the resources in this workbook.

Second, leaders and managers within organizations can use this workbook to improve individual and group performance. When these resources—particularly the assessments, the coaching strategies, and the 100-Day Renewal Project—are used in the context of organizational leadership, it is essential to differentiate coaching from evaluation. These tools are emphatically not to be used for evaluating, rating, comparing, or ranking employees. The purpose of renewal coaching is to create and sustain change for the greater good. This approach helps organizations achieve their goals and assists individuals in reaching performance objectives, but the results of these assessments are never by themselves measurements of organizational or individual performance. If you are a coach within an organization, your roles as evaluator and coach must be rigorously distinct.

Third, if you are not involved in a coaching relationship but want to engage in a process of self-assessment and reflection, this workbook will give you a structured way to proceed.

Fourth, this workbook is the primary resource for participants in Renewal Coaching institutes and seminars. These are conducted exclusively by Douglas Reeves, Elle Allison, and guest Renewal Coaching faculty. To become a licensed renewal coach or to contact a coach suitable to your needs, visit our Web site: www.RenewalCoaching.com

GETTING STARTED: YOUR PERSONAL OBJECTIVES FOR RENEWAL

In every chapter of this workbook we provide space for reflection and guided writing. We begin with a focus on your hopes, dreams, and personal objectives for renewal. We start by asking you to think about your successes and challenges, and then ask you to describe a vision of where you want to be one hundred days from now.

Think of a time in the past when you participated in a successful change either as an individual or as part of a team. Describe the challenge, exactly what you did, and why you think it was successful.

____

____

____

____

What is your greatest challenge right now? Even if this is a long-term challenge that may require months or years of effort, it is important to focus on something that is on your mind as a serious issue at this very moment.

____

____

____

____

What obstacles are preventing you from addressing this challenge? Identify the people, circumstances, resources, or other factors that are adversely affecting your ability to change.

____

____

____

____

____

Look at a calendar and identify the exact date one hundred days from today. Please enter that date here: ____________________

Paint a picture in words of how that day will be different from today if you are able to begin your renewal journey successfully. This does not mean that you will have achieved all of your goals and dreams; but if you are on the road to renewal, describe how you will feel and act differently one hundred days from today.

____

____

____

____

____

SLOW DOWN AND STOP BEFORE YOU SPEED UP

You are now ready to begin, but first, stop for a moment. We know from experience that many readers are voracious learners and tend to speed through as many books as possible, nibbling on a few paragraphs and lurching toward their next quick read. But the same people would never think of listening to their favorite music at three times its regular speed in order to be efficient, nor would they devour a gourmet meal in thirty seconds because it was no more than fuel for their body. They would not, if given the opportunity, go back in history and, while listening to the

Gettysburg Address, ask President Lincoln to pick up the pace and quickly make his point. Your quest for renewal is important. Our words may not be as important as your favorite music or food, and they certainly don't match the eloquence of Lincoln's, but your ideas, your reflections, and your insights certainly are that important. You deserve your own complete attention, and that requires that you slow down, think, and reflect.

PART ONE

Preparation

CHAPTER 1

The Road to Renewal

The *Renewal Coaching Workbook* is designed to be used by professional coaches, their clients (sometimes called "coachees" in the coaching profession), and colleagues within organizations who are seeking to create sustainable change for individuals and team members. The book is divided into four parts: preparation, learning, reflection, and sustaining. Each chapter contains interactive exercises and many opportunities for reflection. Whether you are working alone, with a coach, or in a seminar, each interactive exercise offers valuable insights to help you achieve renewal. At the end of this chapter, there is a special note for professional coaches. If you are participating in a formal Renewal Coaching seminar, then you will complete Part One before the seminar, Part Two during the seminar, and Parts Three and Four after the seminar.

THE SEVEN ELEMENTS OF RENEWAL COACHING

Your journey toward renewal consists of seven elements:

Recognition—Finding patterns of toxicity and renewal

Reality—Confronting change killers in work and life

Reciprocity—Coaching in harmony

Resilience—Coaching through pain

Resonance—Coaching with emotional intelligence

Relationship—Nurturing the personal elements of coaching

Renewal—Creating energy, meaning, and freedom to sustain the journey

For each element of the Renewal Coaching framework you will find assessments to explore your strengths and challenges in each area. Throughout the workbook you will be guided on different paths of reflection that will vary according to your responses to the assessments. Therefore, completing the assessments will be essential for this workbook to be productive for you.

WHY CHANGE FAILS

You already know a great deal about why change fails and succeeds. Think about change efforts that have failed at work or in other organizations in which you have been involved. Consider personal change efforts you have begun with sincerity but, for one reason or another, in which you did not see the results you hoped to achieve. List at least five of these change efforts in the following table along with a few words about why the change effort failed.

Change Effort	Why Change Failed

Now review the changes you listed. What are the common elements of the failure of change based on your own experience?

____

____

____

When we have asked this question of people in seminars around the world, the results have been astonishingly consistent, crossing cultural, economic, and occupational boundaries. Commonly mentioned causes for failure include the following:

"Too much too soon"

"Inadequate buy-in from people who actually had to implement the change"

"Big fanfare followed by no support or implementation"

"Top-down directives without explanation, listening, or empathy"

"Failure to consider the emotional losses associated with change"

These comments are the tip of a very large iceberg of regret and dissatisfaction when people are given the opportunity to discuss why change has failed. Now consider the other side of the equation. Think about change efforts you have seen at work or other organizations that have succeeded. Consider personal change efforts where you saw results over a sustained period of time. List at least five of these change efforts in the following table along with a few words about why each change effort succeeded.

Change Effort	Why Change Succeeded

(continued)

Change Effort	Why Change Succeeded

Now consider the common elements of these successful changes. What do you notice about the reasons for successful change in organizations and in your personal life?

____

____

____

____

____

You have just proven to yourself two things: you know what needs to change and you know why change has failed. Nevertheless, you remain frustrated that individual and organizational change is elusive. You are not alone. With thousands of people in public seminars, we have found many different examples of failed and successful change, but we find one absolutely consistent result: people can list many more failed changes than successful ones, but they are not mystified about the causes. In fact, they are consistently articulate and detailed in their explanations for why change failed. This creates two levels of perplexity. First, with regard to most of the changes, people knew what do to—create better communication at work, employ technology more effectively, make better food selections, treat colleagues kindly, and so on—but their knowledge of what to do was not sufficient to sustain the change. Second, they know why their past change efforts failed. These are insightful and analytical people, just as you are. Therefore, if simply knowing the facts were sufficient, change would not be so difficult. This is why *recognition* is an essential element of Renewal Coaching, but it is only one of the seven elements of the framework. If we have learned anything about sustainable change, it is this compelling and persistent fact: knowledge is not enough. Therefore, you cannot selectively use the chapters from this workbook or the elements of Renewal Coaching as you might select items from the appetizer section of a menu. Every element is critical and interdependent.

USING THIS BOOK ALONE

We know that although the Renewal Coaching community is vibrant and populated with people who will encourage and support you, many people will choose to pursue renewal as a solitary endeavor. If that is the case for you, then consider some guidelines that will be of particular help. First, share your Renewal Coaching pursuits with someone, even if that person is not a coach. Identify a trusted friend, spouse, sibling, or other person whom you trust and tell him or her you are starting an important activity. Say that you have made a decision to seek greater meaning through pursuit of the greater good, even though you may not be entirely sure what that means. Share your frustrations over previous change efforts you have made. Although you do not need to share every reflection you write in this workbook with this confidant (or even with your coach), you do need to make your pursuit of renewal a safe topic of conversation.

Second, gain support from the online community of renewal coaches and clients. The support is free, you can remain completely anonymous, and you will learn powerful and encouraging stories of renewal. You may be inspired to share some of your own. Just go to www.RenewalCoaching.com to participate. There you will find enthusiastic support for your contributions to the greater good. Third, commit to a personal 100-Day Renewal Project. As you will learn, with the proper focus and feedback an enormous amount can be accomplished in a hundred days. Fourth, take the assessments again at the end of your personal journey; you will be able to see measureable progress and thereby reinforce and sustain your efforts.

USING THIS BOOK IN A SEMINAR

If you are enrolled in a Renewal Coaching seminar or certification institute, complete all of the exercises from the Introduction through Chapter Five before the day of the seminar. In addition, please go online to www.RenewalCoaching.com and complete the pre-assessments for each element of the Renewal Coaching framework, print out your results, and bring them with you to the seminar. Start thinking right now about the subject of your 100-Day Renewal Project. This is no casual undertaking but the spark that will give you energy, persistence, and commitment in the weeks and months ahead.

SPECIAL NOTE FOR PROFESSIONAL COACHES

Even if you are an experienced professional coach and intend to use this book and the techniques in it to assist your clients, it is essential that you complete all of the exercises in the workbook. It is a fundamental ethical principle that coaches will not ask clients to engage in activities, assessments, and reflections that the coaches themselves have not first explored in depth. Recent research by the *Harvard Business Review* reveals some startling findings about the coaching profession (Coutu & Kauffman, 2009). First, the reason that people use coaching is shifting dramatically, with survey respondents saying by a wide margin that coaching is used to "develop high potentials or facilitate transition." In the past, the authors conclude, "most companies engaged a coach to help fix toxic behavior at the top. Today, most coaching is about developing the capabilities of high-potential performers" (p. 92).

The complexity and variety of issues you will confront as a coach are also changing. The Renewal Coaching framework places a great deal of emphasis on interpersonal relationships. This emphasis may initially seem irrelevant to some clients. Only 3 percent of coaches in the survey said they were initially engaged to attend primarily to nonwork issues such as work-life balance. However, more than 75 percent of coaches in the study reported addressing personal issues with clients. The plain fact is that even when a coach is engaged by an organization and told to improve organizational effectiveness, the line between the professional and the personal are blurred to the point that the distinction is artificial and unhelpful.

Expert commentary accompanying the Harvard research gave a clarion call to professional coaches for accountability and transparency in their methods. They must be more than a mere sounding board, consultant, or informal advisor. P. Anne Scoular (2009), who teaches coaching at the London Business School, warns, "If a prospective coach can't tell you exactly what methodology he uses—what he does and what outcomes you can expect—show him the door. Top business coaches are as clear about what they don't do as about what they deliver" (p. 96). Although most communications between coach and client are confidential, the Renewal Coaching framework is transparent and should be clearly disclosed to your clients and client organizations.

As a professional coach, you already know the value of an alternative perspective and of integrating alternative systems. You have probably already helped clients to identify the gap between the present and their vision for the future. Equipped with the Renewal Coaching framework, you will add value to your present clients and help get coaching relationships that may be stuck to the next level of productivity and satisfaction. You will have a clearer system for asking questions, providing feedback, and delivering results.

Although we publish our research, case studies, assessments, and ideas in the hope that they will be widely used, it is important to note that the term Renewal Coaching is a service mark protected by domestic and international intellectual property laws and may not be used without the express written permission of Renewal Coaching, LLC. If you are interested in becoming a licensed professional renewal coach, please contact us and we will be happy to assist you.

CHAPTER 2

Are You Ready to Change?

Most people have seen pictures of the Grand Canyon. It's impressive not only in its size but also in some of the terrifying cliffs and narrow trails that only sure-footed mules and indefatigable tourists would traverse. Recently an overlook was built so that visitors can literally walk over the abyss. The floor is transparent so that one can look down at the floor of the Canyon a mile below. If this image does not induce vertigo in the most fearless tourist, then perhaps he or she should consider a career in circus acts such as the high wire or trapeze. The image of walking out over the Grand Canyon, as challenging as it may be for most people, is precisely what we ask of ourselves psychologically when we pursue many change initiatives. We expect to leave the safety of familiar environments and, without even the transparent floor to shield us, we think we can leap across the Grand Canyon borne only by flimsy support, flaccid inspiration, or feckless leaders who employ threats as encouragement to make the leap.

In the previous chapter we explored how much you already know about change—what works, what doesn't, and why change efforts so often fail. We concluded that this state of affairs is not the result of a lack of knowledge: we know what to do. We know the elements of effective and ineffective change, but the chasm between what we know and what we do might as well be the Grand Canyon. In this chapter we explore your readiness for change. This is the essential prerequisite for any coaching engagement, because a resolute resistance to change or even an indifference to it by the client or coach will destroy whatever potential there might have been for success. Indeed, this is precisely the reason that many coaches lapse into the role of consultant rather than coach. It is much easier to offer sage advice than it is to engage in a partnership for meaningful change.

HOW BAD DOES IT HAVE TO GET?

In the literature of addiction and recovery (AA Services, 2001) there is a recurring theme of "hitting bottom," the point at which addicts finally realize they need to seek help. Organizations also hit bottom, sometimes through catastrophic financial results, ethical challenges, or in many unfortunate cases, economic destruction. Like the alcoholic with a fatal liver disease, these organizations recognize their need to change only after it is too late to do so.

Coaches must deal with a complex dichotomy of potential and despair. Many coaching clients are receiving this level of support from their organization because they have been recognized as employees with exceptional potential. At the same time, the organization is seeking help because it faces organizational despair. Inadequate performance, stakeholder dissatisfaction, regulatory threats, and leadership chaos are among the factors that lead exceptionally competent people to need coaching under the most challenging of circumstances. "We have good news and bad news," says the senior manager to the newly promoted leader. "The good news is that you are getting a promotion; the bad news is that you are replacing your former boss, taking on three times the responsibility, and everyone who reports to you resents you for being a survivor of our latest round of layoffs." Wise organizations do not wait for despair and catastrophe to happen before seeking coaching support; instead, they make it part of their culture and required support system. They don't turn the need for coaching on and off any more than they would randomly connect and disconnect the electricity, water, or Internet to and from their offices. No matter how chaotic the outside world is, every individual and organization must have some consistent levels of support.

YOUR PERSONAL HISTORY OF CHANGE

Consider your responses to the inquiries in the previous chapter. You have observed many ineffective changes and perhaps a few effective ones. Now turn the lens inward, from employers and external organizations to yourself. Almost everyone has engaged in some sort of significant change. Perhaps it was positive and voluntary: you decided to improve your health through a regimen of diet and exercise, or you contributed to a significant and personally meaningful team effort at work or in a voluntary capacity. On the other hand, it is possible that your experience with change was involuntary and far from positive: someone you loved died or deeply hurt you, or an employer terminated a position that was linked to your feelings of worth and meaning. Please list your most positive and most negative change experiences in the following table.

Most Positive Changes	Most Negative Changes

Now consider the advantages and disadvantages of these changes. Taking all of them as a whole, identify what you gained and what you lost. Perhaps you gained health and happiness; perhaps you lost both. There is no hidden agenda here—only a request for sincere introspection to learn about your personal experience with change at every level. In the following table, list your losses and gains from the changes you identified in the previous table.

Gains from Change	Losses from Change

What inferences can you draw? Unless your experiences with change have been exceptionally wonderful and you have led a life insulated from the disappointment and anxieties of unexpected and negative change, the inescapable conclusion is that change more often than not is challenging—even when it renders gains. To maximize your chances for changing this pattern, we ask you to engage in the Change Readiness Assessment. You can take this assessment online at www.RenewalCoaching.com or complete it on the following pages. The essence of this assessment is to determine where your readiness for personal change and organizational change intersect. Both of these dynamics are essential and, according to the Harvard study noted in the previous chapter, it is folly for organizations to separate the personal from the professional.

ORGANIZATIONAL CHANGE READINESS ASSESSMENT

This assessment considers the capacity of the organization and the leader to engage in significant change. In the left-hand column, identify three significant changes that have occurred in the organization within the past five years. In each column to the right, enter a score from 0 to 10, with 10 representing the highest level of change effectiveness.

Organizational Change	***Planning:*** **Clear, detailed, effectively communicated**	***Sense of Urgency:*** **Widespread sense of immediate need for change**	***Stakeholder Support:*** **Employees, clients, and community understood and supported change**	***Leadership Focus:*** **Senior leadership made the change their clear and consistent focus long after initiation**	***Impact on Results:*** **The change had a measurable and significant impact on results**
1.					
2.					
3.					

Total for change 1:

Total for change 2:

Total for change 3:

Total for the two highest changes:

PERSONAL CHANGE READINESS ASSESSMENT

Consider three personal changes that you have made in the past five years. These could be a strategic or behavioral change at work or a change in your personal life, such as an improvement in your diet, exercise routine, or personal relationships. Evaluate each change according to the following criteria, scoring from 0 to 10, with 10 representing the highest level of change effectiveness.

Personal Change	***Planning:*** **I planned in advance the steps I would take and knew clearly how to make the change**	***Sense of Urgency:*** **I knew that the price of failing to change was much greater than the price of changing**	***Personal Support:*** **My family and friends knew I was making a change and supported me**	***Personal Focus:*** **I devoted time to initiating and maintaining the change despite my busy schedule**	***Impact on Results:*** **I can measure the results of the change and they are clear and significant**
1.					
2.					
3.					

Total for change 1:

Total for change 2:

Total for change 3:

Total for the two highest changes:

Ready for Learning

An organization can learn from the personal and professional example of a leader who demonstrates a history of successful change, with a strong capacity for planning and execution. Before undertaking a new change initiative, however, the leader must attend to the learning needs of the organization. Specifically, the organization may need to work on planning, communicating, and executing change. Moreover, it must create an evidence-based culture in which a clear and compelling case for change leads to a sense of urgency in every stakeholder. Finally, a commitment to clear and public data displays must be in place so that the results of the change can be widely shared in order to reinforce the commitment and hard work of every person contributing to the change effort.

Ready for Resistance

When neither the leader nor the organization has a history of successful change, the most likely result of any new change initiative will be resistance, anger, and efforts to undermine or simply ignore the effort. Without stakeholder support or leadership execution, these organizations will simply outwait every new change initiative and the leaders who attempt to implement them.

Ready for Frustration

When an organization with a strong history of change is led by someone who is either reluctant to engage in systemic change or lacks the personal capacity to do so, the potential for frustration is high. Each time the organization gets ahead of the leader and the ensuing change fails to be supported by senior leadership, change becomes less safe. Eventually the organization will stop taking risks and migrate to the left-hand side of the Change Readiness Matrix (Figure 2.1). The next leader will inherit an organization with severely compromised change readiness, and it will take time to rebuild trust and regain change capacity.

Ready for Change

When both the leader and the organization have exceptional change capacity, together they are a model of resilience. The organization can adapt to environmental and cultural shifts, change strategies and form, demonstrate innovation in services and resources, and create an atmosphere of excitement and engagement.

THE CHANGE READINESS MATRIX

Examine the Change Readiness Matrix in Figure 2.1 and mark the intersection between organizational change readiness and leadership change readiness using a scale of 0 to 100 for both Organizational Change Capacity and Leadership Change Capacity.

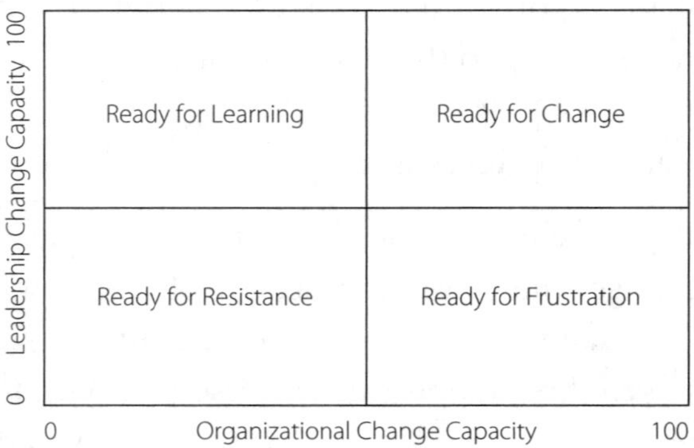

Figure 2.1 Change Readiness Matrix

Note: The point of this is the creation of four broad categories of change readiness, not numerical precision. Therefore, we are not suggesting that there is a statistically meaningful difference between "20 and 30" or between "80 and 90." Rather, we are suggesting that the four categories offer insight into the combination of personal and organizational change readiness. One reason that the vast majority of change initiatives fail is that the effort is begun before leaders have evaluated sufficiently the readiness of their organizations and the people within them to change.

CHAPTER 3

Finding Meaning

Connecting to Your Greater Good

Laney lights up when he talks about his work. When asked about the source of his occupational enthusiasm, he immediately describes his passion for inspiring, motivating, and developing people. He is especially generous in the remarks he makes about the people in the corporation who have mentored and supported him as he has risen through the ranks. He describes the commitment of the company founder, and he fondly names a long list of loyal customers. Presently Laney manages a team whose primary work is to sell protective barrier equipment to businesses such as grocery stores, shipping companies, and industrial plants—anyplace where a moving object or piece of equipment could hit a stable surface. Laney's team sells the protective piece of metal or plastic that prevents significant damage. It is difficult to imagine a more unglamorous industry, and when you hear him talk about his work you struggle to imagine how protective barriers could inspire such passion in a young man—until you realize that Laney is so inspired not because he believes protective barriers will save the world but because he really loves developing and supporting the sales team he leads.

Laney's passion is contagious and his team has exceeded financial goals every quarter. Yet Laney is equally if not more proud of other indicators that represent success as far as he is concerned. These indicators include the percentages of team members who work together to make a sale, of repeat clients who rate their interaction with the sales force as a perfect 10, of innovative sales strategies conceived and executed by his team, and of team members who have been with the company for three or more years. But there is an even more important reason for Laney's passion, and his eyes glitter and dance around as he gets to this part of his story: his sales team is drawn forward to exceed its goals because when it does the company donates 15 percent of these funds to the local community arts program for kids.

There is more to Laney's story. If Laney saw himself as just a manager in a company that sells protective barriers, he might be just another working stiff, shuffling back and forth between home and office, counting the days to each vacation and marking time to the year he finally retires. But Laney's work has profound meaning for him. The intensity with which he creates and sustains relationships that empower others belies a deeper importance for Laney—even deeper than being able to exceed goals and contribute to the community arts program. The story Laney will continue to tell you, if you ask, is about his older brother who died when they were just kids.

As a seven-year-old, Laney worshipped his big brother. When his brother passed away, Laney was heartbroken. Although he was a small boy, he understood he had prematurely lost a precious relationship. He also understood that people mean everything, relationships mean everything. As he grew up, the resilient Laney turned every experience into an opportunity to form and nurture relationships. Over time he discovered he had a knack for this, which in turn contributed to his success as manager of a sales force. Once you hear Laney's whole story, you realize he has a strong sense about his purpose on this planet. He seeks to fill a need that transcends any individual or organizational desire to meet financial goals and achieve stability in work and life. Laney uses his work to redeem the loss of his brother and energize a force for a greater good, one that builds strong relationships and empowers all involved to make life better for others.

Reflection on Laney's Story

As you were reading about Laney, were you reminded of anything in your own life? Maybe you felt a rush of regret or anxiety because you don't feel about your work and life the way Laney does. Or maybe you felt kinship with Laney because you also feel you are doing work that matters and that you are perhaps even "meant to do." Or maybe you have been harboring thoughts about work or projects at your current workplace that would provide meaning for you. Use the space below to record your thoughts so far.

Laney's story made me feel this about my own life:

I resonate with Laney because:

I do not resonate with Laney because:

WHAT MAKES A GREATER GOOD?

Past president of the American Psychological Association, Robert Sternberg (2000), is a leading expert and prolific writer on the topic of wisdom. Sternberg associates wisdom with what he calls the common good and what we call the greater good. Sternberg proposes that the common good is the result of wisdom in action. The common good is seen in solutions and decisions that go beyond self-interest to consider what is also good for others and the environment, "such as one's city or country or environment or even God" (p. 638). The nature of wisdom in individuals may be difficult to describe, but it is usually recognized in the way a person faces dilemmas and adversity and ultimately responds to them. This is one reason that the greater good is not only essential to renewal but also makes it a perfect fit with models of coaching. Good coaching is almost always about supporting others to achieve something remarkable. The greater good is remarkable because it always goes beyond the usual to-do list of the individual to consider the perspectives and needs of others, and it results in a visible action, process, product, or artifact that makes life better for stakeholders, shareholders, and the general population at large.

THE GREATER GOOD IN ORGANIZATIONS

Inspired by a desire to win back public confidence and trust, values that were lost in an avalanche of financial scandals and short-term corporate greed, students from the 2009 graduating class of Harvard Business School created the MBA Oath (http://mbaoath.org/take-the-oath). It opens with this paragraph:

> As a manager, my purpose is to serve the greater good by bringing people and resources together to create value that no single individual can create alone. Therefore I will seek a course that enhances the value my enterprise can create for society over the long term. I recognize my decisions can have far-reaching consequences that affect the well-being of individuals inside and outside my enterprise, today and in the future.

The MBA Oath has become a great conversation starter in the global business and economic community. Some businesspeople have embraced the idea of a code of ethics for managers; others feel that the code unfairly implies that most or even all managers seek profit at all costs. In truth, organizations and businesses that are working toward a greater good abound. These are the tremendous men and women who turn a social profit along with a financial profit. They include entrepreneurs such as Judy Wicks, who founded White Dog Cafe in Philadelphia to create local living communities that emphasize healthy food, living wage jobs, and support for minority business development. They are private companies like Google, committed to for-profit philanthropy, and Weight Watchers, which held a "Lose for Good" program in which for every pound lost by participating members over a six-week period a matching pound of food was donated to domestic and international food banks. They include SC Johnson—the company that makes cleaning products—which ironically built one of their manufacturing plants strategically near a garbage dump so they could harness the methane gas from the garbage to power their equipment. And they are the nonprofit organizations—really the social entrepreneurs of the world—aligning their strategies to whatever mission they seek to fulfill day to day for the good of society and our planet.

They are also individuals and organizations that you don't see in the news. They are "regular" people who have either created or uncovered a greater good in the work they do and in the lives they lead—people like Brandon, a talented young hair stylist who told Elle, "I love my work because whenever you have the privilege of touching another person, as a hair designer does, you have a responsibility. For the time the person is in your chair, you can treat them with special care—and that may be the only special treatment they receive in their lives."

Although frameworks for corporate social responsibility call for systemwide strategies in order to do well and do good, we don't have one thing in mind when we talk about the greater good. Within the context of the Renewal Coaching framework, the actual greater good selected by a client or organization is uniquely subjective, often either directly related to or tangential to the core mission and purpose of the business or organization. It is what draws individuals and organizations forward in any change process, even when the going gets rough or the work is unglamorous. As we saw in the case of Laney, one individual within an organization may champion a specific greater good, or an individual within an organization may pursue the greater good even when others do not, as Renaldo, a Bay Area engineer in the computer chip business, did when he decided singlehandedly to recycle paper from the offices. What energizes Renaldo is whatever he can do to contribute to a healthy planet. In the beginning, his coworkers saw him as a peculiar character they needed to humor. But after two years, more and more of Renaldo's coworkers save their recyclable paper, because they know that every Friday, on his own time, he comes around to collect it.

Pursuit of the greater good has never meant rejection of creating wealth and profit. As Margaret Rode, founder of Websites for Good, told us, "If you aren't making any money, you won't be around to do much of any good for anyone." Savitz and Weber, authors of *The Triple Bottom Line: How Today's Best-Run Companies Are Achieving Economic, Social, and Environmental Success—and How You Can Too* (2006) would agree. In their book they cite companies that have found what they tag the "sustainability sweet spot," where every decision is made with regard for both profit and people. They suggest that this intersection of creating outcomes that are good for shareholders and those that are also good for stakeholders is what every company that wants to remain in business over the long haul should strive for.

UNCOVERING YOUR PERSONAL GREATER GOOD

It is tempting to rely on external signs from the universe to tell us what we are meant to do with our lives, but this passive approach to finding personal meaning is a thin disguise at best, for procrastination, and at worst, for living a small, safe life. Some people wait forever for someone else to step in, discover their talents and passions, and tell them what their lives are all about. Other people die waiting for the perfect sign from the heavens that "this" is what they were born to do, all the while blaming a higher power for the miserable life they wake up to day to day. Still others know what they are meant to do but are simply too afraid, too distracted, or too lazy to follow through.

There is a better, more proactive, more optimistic way. It's in the spirit of holocaust survivor and psychotherapist Viktor Frankl, who tells us that *we* must actively seek and name the meaning in our lives rather than wait for someone outside ourselves to hand it to us. Renewal Coaching demands a proactive stance toward living a meaningful life. It begins with searching your own heart for what gives you meaning.

This chapter will lead you through several exercises to help you uncover and name the meaning in your life. Once you know and understand what gives you personal meaning, then the greater good, and even multiple kinds of greater good, will become apparent to you. Like Laney, you will uncover what transforms the suffering in your life into renewal so that you can achieve outcomes through the work you do that make a difference for people and the planet, and also make a profit.

For those of you who work or volunteer in a business or organization, the greater good might be found within the existing mission and structures of the system, or it might require innovation and ingenuity—the creation of something new. Perhaps an opportunity to serve the greater good will emerge in processes and policies that better support the employees within the organization itself or people within the surrounding community. Be open to looking at all ideas that come up as you continue working with this chapter.

BEGIN WITH LOSS

That which has caused us pain is a powerful source of energy in our lives. As Buddhist teacher Pema Chodron said in a conversation with Margaret Wheatley (1999), "It surprises us that the darkness is a source of inspiration." As confounding as it may be to identify a greater good by starting with what has caused us suffering, the truth is, our losses beg redemption, and redemption always points the way to something better.

Reflect on your past losses by linking them to the present. Consider first the example of Belinda, a division vice president of a European car manufacturing company with plants in North and South America, presented in the following table:

Belinda's Example

The Present: My current interests, passions, skills, talents, positions, and roles		The Past: Losses in my life, big and small
1. I am part of a cross-country hiking club. 2. I earned a business degree and specialize in guiding organizational change. 3. I love animals and take my two dogs to the neighborhood dog park each day. 4. I put up a profile on a professional social networking site and am teaching my friends and coworkers how to maximize its use. 5. Our family takes one cooking class each month together. 6. I volunteer at the community food pantry. 7. I control my own investments and have a plan to grow them within a balanced portfolio. 8. I bought my own house and furnished it with great finds from the flea market, eBay, Craigslist, and garage sales. My rule is recycle, reuse, reduce!		1. My dad lost his job when I was twelve and the family had an extended period of financial hardship. 2. My twin sister was put into a different kindergarten than me and I got to see her only during recess. 3. I flunked a math class my freshman year of college. 4. My first boyfriend dumped me for a girl down the street and I had to find a new way to walk home from school so I didn't run into them. 5. My husband and I moved from the community we lived in for fifteen years and I left behind the friends I knew from high school. 6. My position at work changed to include responsibilities I had never held before. 7. My car was stolen. 8. Our son got a DUI the first time we let him drive the family car after he got his driver's license.

Belinda drew several arrows between the two columns. Before doing this exercise, she did not realize that many of the talents, skills, interests, and assets she had developed in her life stemmed from a challenging and character-forming childhood experience. The power of recognizing the origins of many of her passions in life is that she now has insight about what she finds meaningful and about where she might be able to give back in ways that transform the work she does from "just a job" into something with significance.

Now you try:

Step 1: Recall all of the events in your life that count as loss for you and list them as you think of them in the right-hand column of the following table. They can be anything from the loss of a loved one, a relationship, a job, a pet, a home or neighborhood, your health, or even a cherished belief or illusion. Losses are subjective. No one can judge the depth of a loss for another person.

Step 2: Once you complete this list, in the left-hand column list all of your current interests, passions, skills, and talents, and positions you have had or roles you have played.

Step 3: Now, in the center column, draw lines of connection between the items in the two lists. Can you trace any of the items from the left column (the present) back in time (the past) to a loss in the right-hand column? It is okay if several items from the left connect to the same item on the right. It is also okay if the connection is vague or remote. What matters is that you feel a connection exists.

The Present: My current interests, passions, skills, talents, positions, and roles		**The Past: Losses in my life, big and small**

Next, among the losses that are connected to the life you are leading in the present, circle those that "call out to you," that is, those whose influence in your life you are developing a new awareness of. They may or may not be the losses with the greatest number of arrows pointing to them. List them here:

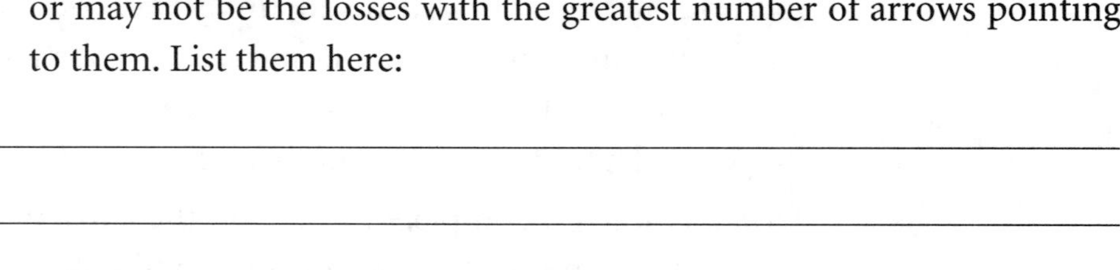

For each of the losses you listed, brainstorm all the ways you can imagine that a person could redeem them, that is, take some kind of action that is directly related to the issue, in your work or in your personal life. In brainstorming, all possible ideas are generated without censoring them or evaluating them for what is feasible or practical. Write down every idea you think of even if you can't imagine yourself doing it. You can include the things you already do that are connected.

For example, Belinda's brainstorm might look like this:

Loss: Our son got a DUI the first time he drove the family car
Redemption brainstorm in work and life: Continue with the family cooking class each month to strengthen the relationship we have with our son. Initiate network of families of teen drivers in the neighborhood to create unified monitoring of parties and driving. Start a "safe ride program" in my community and donate vehicles from the plant for the fleet. Become involved in Mothers Against Drunk Driving and start a chapter at our son's high school. Start a teen volunteer program to deliver meals to homebound seniors.

Loss: My husband and I moved from the community we lived in for fifteen years and I left behind the friends I knew from high school
Redemption brainstorm in work and life: Institute an international welcome committee at each manufacturing plant. Celebrate the anniversary of the date that each person joined the company. Support social networks within the company by providing matching funding streams for clubs and hobby groups. Institute a mentor program for each new hire. Prepare and provide a welcome kit for the families of new hires and those relocating to work in the company. Set up a communications room in each plant so employees and family members can Skype relatives and families who are out of state or in a different country.

Loss: My dad lost his job when I was twelve and the family had an extended period of financial hardship
Redemptive brainstorm in work and life: Set up a college scholarship fund for children of employees. Establish a car donation system to benefit nonprofits. Create an onsite or community university at our largest plants where workers can complete their GED. Offer financial planning counseling to employees and their families. Require each division to provide work experience opportunities for local high school students as part of their annual budgets.

Your turn:

Loss:
Redemptive Brainstorm:
Loss:
Redemptive Brainstorm:
Loss:
Redemptive Brainstorm:

After you complete this exercise, take a moment to reflect on any themes that emerged in the brainstorm. As you read your list, notice which of the brainstormed ideas makes you feel excited, optimistic, and inventive, and really makes you smile when you think about making it happen. These emotions are indicators that you are discovering or affirming what is meaningful to you personally. Write down your "greater good" ideas here:

____

____

____

____

____

A Compelling Vision of the Greater Good

Now that you have identified one or more greater-good ideas, write a paragraph or two to describe fully what will be possible for others and for the larger context (the environment of the organization, your family, your communities). Describe the benefits this year, three years out, five years out, ten years out, and beyond the next generation. Describe what you will be doing. Describe the impact on people, planet, and profits.

____

____

____

____

____

____

____

____

____

____

____

____

Team and Organizational Greater Good

Work teams and organizations can complete these exercises together. Coaches and coaching leaders can approach this process either by having individuals work through the exercises on their own and then discussing their responses together, or by completing the exercises together from the perspective of the whole team or organization. If you choose the latter option, the group will list actions and losses of the team or organization and then brainstorm all of the possibilities for the group. Take care to explore fully the benefits to the organization from the perspective of both shareholders and stakeholders.

A Lifetime of Greater Good

The greater good is what sustains change initiatives. Without the greater good, individuals and teams may feel personally satisfied and may meet quarterly objectives and annual goals, but they will lack the opportunity to understand the significance of those outcomes for people beyond the obvious benefactors. In the absence of a greater good, work becomes just work. Given the number of hours most people give to their work over a lifetime, the greater good is not an indulgent luxury or just a by-product of those who have "do-gooder" impulses. No, it is primary to the sustenance of humanity.

IF YOUR LIFE IS THE ANSWER, WHAT IS THE QUESTION?

Ultimately, the essence of our lives, who we are at our core, is an answer to a question that is even larger than the greater good itself. Any one person's or organization's greater good is, after all, just one manifestation of the answer to the needs on this wonderful planet. Many of us are simultaneously responding to the same needs we see around us, whether the need for a cure for cancer or for the uplifting of a spirit, but we do so with our unique gifts, fueled by the experiences of our lives, including the losses and adversities that have honed and refined our character. Each minute, hour, day, and year illuminates the answer to the unique question that begs for what we will do with our lives to provide a response. Here are some examples of Life Questions:

- How do people become so extraordinary that they are capable of achieving everything they dream of?
- How does a society remove barriers that diminish the power of a person?
- Why does it matter that people feel connected and know they are not alone?
- How does a complex, global society take care of the planet?
- How do we shepherd the next generation of humans into the new technologies of the world?

What is the question that your life answers?

____

____

____

____

____

PART TWO

Learning

CHAPTER 4

Pre-Assessment

Finding Your Strengths and Challenges

Renewal Coaching is a feedback-intensive reflective process. In other coaching models, much of the feedback comes from other people. For example, 360-degree feedback is a standard part of many leadership coaching models, and psychological assessment is integral to therapeutic models of coaching. In Renewal Coaching, by contrast, the client is the author and analyst of the feedback. In this chapter, you will conduct a complete pre-assessment using a separate assessment for each element of Renewal Coaching: recognition, reality, reciprocity, resilience, resonance, relationship, and renewal. Please do not expect to "do well" on these assessments. In fact, the assessments are designed deliberately to confound people who want to "do well." Sometimes the optimal score is high, sometimes it is low, and sometimes it is in the middle. Therefore, just provide authentic responses and challenge yourself to be ruthlessly honest.

If you have access to a computer, please use it to complete the seven assessments at www.RenewalCoaching.com. If you do not have access to a computer, then please complete these assessments by hand. Each assessment has two parts: the objective (responding to questions on a 1 to 10 scale) and the subjective (writing out extended responses to questions). Remember, give yourself a break; you are at the beginning of the program, not at the end, so don't demand perfection. We have both been teachers and we have always been surprised at students and parents who have expressed astonishment when we have told them they were not doing what we thought they were capable of in September. So many successful students, who later become successful adults, have always been told that they are nearly perfect. When a teacher is willing to challenge that presumption, these students plaintively ask, "But you are saying I'm not doing everything right!" We reply gently, lovingly, and clearly, "That's correct—*that's why you go to school.*" That is precisely where you are right now. You are about to receive some feedback that suggests that you are less than perfect, that you have room for improvement—the curse of most performance reviews from the executive suite to kindergarten. Who could possibly bear the burden of the label "needs improvement" except the most wretched failures? In fact, the label "needs improvement" applies to only one group: honest people. We hope that this label and its association with honesty and integrity apply to the readers of this workbook. If they do apply to you, then please read on or take the online assessments.

Recognition Assessment

For a computerized administration of this assessment, log on to www.RenewalCoaching.com, then select Assessment.

Date:

Stage of Renewal Coaching

- Not started
- In progress—3 months
- In progress—6 months
- In progress—9 months
- In progress—12 or more months

Instructions: Respond to each of the following statements quickly, providing your first impulse as the answer. A response of 10 is the strongest possible agreement, and 1 is the strongest possible disagreement. There are no correct answers. However, the assessment will be most useful to you if you provide the most authentic response, and that is likely to be the first response that comes to mind.

Statement	Strongly Disagree → Strongly Agree
1. Once I've come to a conclusion, I tend to stick with it. In fact, most of the conclusions about people and about life that I came to in high school and college are still true today.	1 2 3 4 5 6 7 8 9 10
2. I keep my life pretty compartmentalized. I'm one person at work, another person at home, and a different person when I'm involved in community activities.	1 2 3 4 5 6 7 8 9 10
3. Even though the world situation has changed in the past few years, the plain fact is that global politics haven't changed much. The things I knew ten years ago are still true today.	1 2 3 4 5 6 7 8 9 10
4. When I think about the different jobs I have had, my work habits and personal relationship patterns have changed with each job. Different communities, bosses, and organizations bring out different behaviors in me.	1 2 3 4 5 6 7 8 9 10
5. When I think about customer service, it's just a universally awful experience. It doesn't make any difference if it's the airlines, restaurants, or the Girl Scout cookie sale—you just can't get any kind of customer service any more.	1 2 3 4 5 6 7 8 9 10

Recognition Assessment (continued)

Statement	Strongly Disagree → Strongly Agree
6. Although my friends make a big deal out of the differences among Apple, IBM, and other brand names, most technology is pretty much the same.	1 2 3 4 5 6 7 8 9 10
7. Let's face it—there are dog people and there are cat people, and they are fundamentally different based on the sort of animals they prefer.	1 2 3 4 5 6 7 8 9 10
8. Kids today are really different—disrespect, tattoos, piercings, texting—they seem as if they're from a different planet than when I was in school.	1 2 3 4 5 6 7 8 9 10
9. I've learned that people who work hard are always more successful, and that when people are not successful, it's because they didn't work hard enough.	1 2 3 4 5 6 7 8 9 10
10. Women and men? It's not just Mars and Venus—it's different galaxies. There are just some universal qualities that apply to women, and very different characteristics that apply to men.	1 2 3 4 5 6 7 8 9 10

Total score: ________

10–40	You are remarkably resistant to overgeneralization. That's a good thing, as you resist prejudice, bigotry, and inappropriate inferences from limited evidence. At the same time, you might be so equivocal that you resist any conclusion, even when the evidence is clear. Perhaps you are waiting for evidentiary perfection, a standard that courts do not apply even in the death penalty. When the stakes are lower, you might benefit from a willingness to draw inferences from reasonable evidence, but evidence that is short of perfection.
41–70	You provide a thoughtful blend of skepticism and reason. Although you are not willing to make sweeping generalizations when they are not warranted by the available evidence, you are also not afraid to express some hypotheses suggested by the available data. You are willing to be proved wrong; in fact, you probably have been proved wrong by your spouse, kids, and coworkers. You don't regard that as a mark of shame, but only the result of a healthy willingness to gather information, analyze it, and express some ideas based on it. When other evidence comes along that challenges your previous conclusions, you are

Recognition Assessment (continued)

	willing to supplant your previous conclusions with those that are supported by evidence that is better and more recent. Sometimes you are surprised by what you've learned in the past ten years; other times you are equally surprised by how smart and insightful your grandparents were, and how little things have changed. In the end, it's evidence, not tradition, that guides your thinking.
71–100	You have a degree of certainty that is matched only by Alex Trebek and Mr. Spock. Trebek has all of the answers, thanks to the producers of *Jeopardy*, and Spock has no emotions to interfere with his rational abilities. You don't need to be bothered with a lot of evidence, as you are able to draw certain conclusions with only a couple of examples. This certitude serves you well in some cases—people love it when you exude confidence in public speaking and your bosses appreciate your sense of self-confidence. Your colleagues, however, are often skeptical of your claims. When they challenge you, particularly in a public meeting, you tend to become angry and flustered, particularly if they ask you for data to support your conclusions. There are times when, in the deepest and most private parts of your mind, you wonder if your certainty is justified. But these moments pass quickly, as you substitute doubt with conviction. After all, people depend on you, and they expect you to be right all of the time, and you can't let them down.

Open Response Assessment

Complete each of these open-ended questions, being attentive to trends and patterns that suggest reactions that are not related to a single situation but that are a reflection of your consistent personal beliefs and behaviors.

1. When you start something new, what do you tend to do first? Do you picture what it will look like when it is accomplished and describe it for others or do you immediately think about the steps it will take to execute the project?

____

____

____

____

____

Recognition Assessment (continued)

2. Would others agree with how you responded to the second question?

____

3. Think of a group you belong to that is important to you such as your family, your work team, or your organization. What are you known for within this group? (Here are some examples: I get things done, I'm the devil's advocate, I bring up new ideas, I'm quiet, I disagree often.)

____

____

4. When you are under stress and you have to make decisions under less than ideal situations, how do you respond? Do you become more engaged or do you withdraw? Do you feel hopeful or do you feel powerless? What do you intend to accomplish with your response?

____

____

____

____

____

5. Think of a time when you responded to a difficult situation in a way consistent with how others see you. What was the outcome? Now think of a similar situation but where you responded differently from your usual manner. What happened?

____

____

____

____

____

____

____

____

Recognition Assessment (continued)

6. Think of a time when you responded to a difficult situation in a manner consistent with the expectations of the organization. What was the outcome? If you wished you could have responded differently, would you have done so? What risks would be inherent to responding differently? What benefits could have resulted?

7. Recall an occasion when you knew your response to the emotions and behaviors of others could either improve a difficult situation or make it worse. What did you decide to do? What was the outcome?

8. Think of a day or several hours in the past week when you felt you made decisions that "worked" for the situation you found yourself in. Describe the events of that day. Focus on the following four areas:
   a. What was on your schedule that day that was good for you personally in the present (for example, went for a run, listened to my favorite music, met with my coach, had breakfast with my spouse and settled our weekend plans)?

Recognition Assessment (continued)

b. What was on your schedule that supported you in building your personal preferred future (for example, taking a class in the latest technology, attending toastmasters, writing a professional article, updating your website)?

c. What was on your schedule that day that supported others right now (for example, training for others so they feel competent and confident, conversations that remove barriers, events that elicit or showcase multiple perspectives and successes)?

d. What was on your schedule that day that related to support for others and the greater good (for example, recognition of indicators of success that go beyond the bottom line, decisions that clearly benefit the needs of others beyond yourself)?

9. What emotional patterns are you sick and tired of in yourself because they cause you pain and make you want to just get through your day when they become issues? For example, you know you always overreact to anything less than perfect; you know you always withdraw and avoid confrontation when people disagree with you—even on things that are important to you; you know you always try to accommodate others.

___

___

10. What emotional and behavioral patterns consistently make events turn out well for you and for others concerned (for example, admitting error, face-to-face communication, taking action, including others, assuming positive presuppositions, wanting others to succeed, recognizing others, considering the merits in others' perspectives)?

___

___

Reality Assessment

For a computerized administration of this assessment, log on to www.RenewalCoaching.com, then select Assessment.

Date:

Stage of Renewal Coaching

- Not started
- In progress—3 months
- In progress—6 months
- In progress—9 months
- In progress—12 or more months

Instructions: Respond to each of the following statements qu ckly, providing your first impulse as the answer. A response of 10 is the strongest possible agreement, and 1 is the strongest possible disagreement. There are no correct answers. However, the assessment will be most useful to you if you provide the most authentic response, and that is likely to be the first response that comes to mind.

Statement	**Strongly Disagree → Strongly Agree**
1. Whenever I hear claims from coworkers about their job performance, I tend to doublecheck the facts.	1 2 3 4 5 6 7 8 9 10
2. When salespeople tell me the price of an item, it's just their bargaining position, not the real price.	1 2 3 4 5 6 7 8 9 10
3. When my romantic partners have told me about their successes, they are probably just trying to impress me.	1 2 3 4 5 6 7 8 9 10
4. When a doctor or other health professional recommends a treatment, I always get a second opinion and check out additional information for myself.	1 2 3 4 5 6 7 8 9 10
5. If a colleague asks me for help on a project, it probably means that he or she is a poor time manager.	1 2 3 4 5 6 7 8 9 10
6. If a client or customer says that he or she will work out the written details of a contract at a later date, it means that this person intends to change our verbal agreement.	1 2 3 4 5 6 7 8 9 10
7. When I receive a compliment from a supervisor or coworker, they are just flattering me to make me feel good and not giving me an accurate indication of their real opinions.	1 2 3 4 5 6 7 8 9 10

Reality Assessment (continued)

Statement	Strongly Disagree → Strongly Agree
8. If I ask my staff for critical feedback about the results of a project and they say that everything is fine, then they are probably just covering up for poor work and not leveling with me.	1 2 3 4 5 6 7 8 9 10
9. When I received praise from teachers or parents, they were just trying to make me feel good and not really complimenting my performance.	1 2 3 4 5 6 7 8 9 10
10. When people in our community ask me to volunteer to take a leadership role or participate in a community activity, it means that they must be very desperate and have had several other people say no.	1 2 3 4 5 6 7 8 9 10

Total score: ________

10–40	You are without question a delightful and friendly person, but you may not reach the next chapter of this book because you are likely to lend your copy to your brother-in-law who has not returned the last ten books he borrowed. You are so trusting that you are sometimes gullible, accepting statements from friends, colleagues, and family members that have little factual support. You may be secretly angry with yourself for being taken advantage of so much in the past, but you continue to accept the statements and behavior of other people without critical analysis because you hope that someday your experience will be proven correct. In your coaching work, you should seek ways to identify instances in which you have been misled and rehearse practical and appropriate ways to challenge others. You don't want to become a cynic, but you are tired of being a doormat.
41–70	You have a nuanced view of reality. You've given up on the tooth fairy, but not necessarily on good fortune and the occasional miracle that life has to offer. You are appropriately skeptical when people or organizations have proved themselves untrustworthy, but you also give colleagues, friends, and family the benefit of the doubt. You are particularly helpful in meetings, where you provide a combination of support for new and challenging ideas while not accepting obvious bluster and unsupportable assertions without a request for evidence. Look for organizational roles in which your thoughtful perspective can be shared with others. Don't be afraid to challenge the perpetual skeptics who kill new ideas. Take time to encourage those who might have the ability to engage in critical thinking but rarely express that skill publicly.

Reality Assessment (continued)

71–100 You may have had some friends describe you as cynical, distrustful, and a person whose expectations are regularly met because you expect the worst and are therefore not disappointed. Your colleagues and friends know that they have to be on their toes around you, because you are quick to challenge whatever they say. Of course, there do not seem to be many colleagues and friends having conversations with you these days, as they carefully avoid any repetitions of their previous unpleasant confrontations with you. You may be the boss of your organization; perhaps you think that you achieved this status because of your "critical thinking," but your colleagues (and probably your family and friends) just see you as critical. If you want to help your colleagues and yourself be happier and more successful, then try going for a full day without a single verbal stiletto, e-mail flame, or other public attempt to show the world how superior you are. You may have to lose a very important job or relationship before you take this feedback seriously.

Open Response Assessment

In order to help clients become more successful, coaches must help them develop a reality orientation. The Reality Assessment for Clients is a good start to this process, but it is by nature abstract and not necessarily related to the daily reality of the client. A much more serious assessment of reality should take place in every coaching conversation as the coach and client consider extended responses to the questions here. They are a source of reflection for coaching conversations. It is the responsibility of the coach to address reality not only in the client's work relationships but also in the coaching relationship. These focus questions will assist the coach:

1. What data and other indicators have you brought to our conversation today?

____

____

____

2. When you say "everybody" or "many people," can you be specific with regard to the names and numbers of people whom you are describing?

____

____

____

Reality Assessment (continued)

3. What other perspectives have you considered in reaching this point of view?

4. Who else might have a different point of view on this matter?

5. Whose advice should you seek? Consider in particular people from whom you have not previously requested their point of view. Consider also people at different levels of the organization and different parts of the organization. Consider people from different walks of life, different traditions, different cultures, and different life experiences.

6. How would you express the same idea in a way that considers more than a single conclusion?

7. The data clearly show a certain result, and you believe that you know the cause of that result. What other causes might have caused or contributed to the same result?

Reality Assessment (continued)

8. If you could change this situation in any way you wanted, what would that be?

9. What do you need to learn in order to better understand this situation? What is the most recent information that you have? Would it help you understand the situation better if you seek updated data?

10. What is your emotional history with this matter? When you think about it, do you feel anxiety, anger, stress, satisfaction, pleasure, fear, gratitude, or other emotional reactions? How do those reactions influence your analysis and conclusions? How would you see the situation differently if you purposely adopted a different emotional perspective?

Reciprocity Assessment

For a computerized administration of this assessment, log on to www.RenewalCoaching.com, then select Assessment.

Date:

Stage of Renewal Coaching

- Not started
- In progress—3 months
- In progress—6 months
- In progress—9 months
- In progress—12 or more months

Instructions: Respond to each of the following statements quickly, providing your first impulse as the answer. A response of 10 is the strongest possible agreement, and 1 is the strongest possible disagreement. There are no correct answers. However, the assessment will be most useful to you if you provide the most authentic response, and that is likely to be the first response that comes to mind.

Statement	Strongly Disagree → Strongly Agree
1. Whenever I'm asked to help for a community charitable event, I always say yes, even if I don't really have the time.	1 2 3 4 5 6 7 8 9 10
2. When my colleagues ask for help on a task that is undefined and vague, my immediate reaction is to say yes, and I don't really need to ask for clarity.	1 2 3 4 5 6 7 8 9 10
3. When I have a challenge at work, I can work through it myself. I rarely or ever need to ask for help or support.	1 2 3 4 5 6 7 8 9 10
4. When my supervisor gives me an assignment, I have never suggested that I was overloaded, even if I was swamped with work at that time.	1 2 3 4 5 6 7 8 9 10
5. When my work is not getting done, I just grind it out. I can pull an all-nighter now as well as I did in college.	1 2 3 4 5 6 7 8 9 10
6. When I notice a need in a different part of my organization, I routinely jump in and get the job done. It's faster and easier to do it myself than ask them to do it.	1 2 3 4 5 6 7 8 9 10

Reciprocity Assessment (continued)

Statement	Strongly Disagree → Strongly Agree
7. I'd rather work alone than ask colleagues for help.	1 2 3 4 5 6 7 8 9 10
8. When something needs to be done around the house, I just fix it, even if my spouse or kids were supposed to be responsible for it.	1 2 3 4 5 6 7 8 9 10
9. When I'm stuck in a project or assignment, I'd rather go to the Web for help than ask my colleagues.	1 2 3 4 5 6 7 8 9 10
10. When a task or project isn't getting done, it's not my fault. I'm just buried in other work that people have assigned to me and everybody knows that I'm always overloaded.	1 2 3 4 5 6 7 8 9 10

Total score: ________

10–15 "It is better to receive than give" appears to be your motto, and this formula may have worked well for you in the past. In fact, it works particularly well if you are used to serial relationships at work and in your personal life, where other people seem at first to enjoy offering you assistance and, just before they grow weary of the asymmetrical nature of your relationship, you move on to the next company, team, friend, lover, or spouse. After all, you perform best as a solo player, and everybody else seems to benefit as well. If there's a tough shot at the end of the game, pass the ball to you and you'll take it, owning the game ball that was delivered to you by unsung teammates. Tough presentation to management or a key customer? You'll take twenty-five of the available thirty minutes, even if a team of twelve put the presentation together. Ultimately, however, the world is a small place, and your reputation will precede you. Nobody is asking you to be a chump or to let others take advantage of you, but it's time to pitch in and help someone else for a change. Take notes in the next meeting, write the report that will have other people's names on it, make the bed, stack the dishwasher, turn off the television, and initiate a conversation. We're probably not the first people to tell you these things, so it may be necessary for you to lose something very important to you before you realize that the people who first told you to share—your mother, kindergarten teacher, or teammate—were probably right.

Reciprocity Assessment (continued)

16–70	You have a healthy and rare balance between giving and taking, knowing that you have to do a bit of both to maximize your effectiveness. You appear to understand the nature of reciprocity, helping others while being able to accept help graciously and consistently. You have probably noticed that people from whom you accept assistance are happy to provide it, knowing that they can count on you as well. Because your balanced-state sense of reciprocity is rare, don't take it for granted. It is very easy to slip into the giver mode, so challenge yourself regularly to look for patterns that tend to make the giver or taker extreme.
71–100	You might be reading this while waiting for a colleague, sibling, spouse, child, parent, or complete stranger, all of whom you have volunteered to help, even though they keep you waiting, abuse your time, focus solely on themselves, and all the while are confident that they are doing you a favor by allowing you to help them. If the child you are waiting on is two and a half years old or younger, then she gets a pass. She is not a tyrant and you are not seeking sainthood—it's just what infants and toddlers need. In every other case, however, it's time to reevaluate the nature of your giving and their taking. Even if you have taken vows of poverty, obedience, and promiscuity, all designed to meet the needs of others, the truth is that you are not helping people by eternal self-sacrifice. They will never learn to be what you want them to be—an equal partner in a relationship with you—until you give up the martyrdom of unequal service and support. At the Ritz-Carlton Hotels, the service staff—the people who clean rooms, make beds, serve coffee, and vacuum the carpets—know from their first day on the job that they are "ladies and gentlemen serving ladies and gentlemen." No matter what their job or how apparently menial their service, they have dignity and respect, because they know that they remain ladies and gentlemen. Can you say the same as a result of the many, many services you are rendering? Try this experiment for the next thirty days. Don't pick up other people's coffee cups after the next staff meeting (you didn't think that we were watching?). Don't make the beds of your teenagers. Don't pick up your spouse's socks (yes, we're watching him or her too). The next time you write a report for a colleague, ask clearly, respectfully, and firmly that your name appear on the document as the author. Practice these words: "I would like" and "I prefer not to." The most important phrase for you to start using is, "I already have a commitment," even if that commitment is to yourself for some time alone. When your stunned colleague, child, spouse, or friend starts to insist, saying that you have always cooperated in the past, don't provide a lecture on how you will no longer put up with their self-centered abuse. Don't give a lecture on the essential symbiotic nature of reciprocity. Just say, "No thanks. I've got another commitment."

Reciprocity Assessment (continued)

Open Response Assessment

Complete each of these open-ended questions, being attentive to trends and patterns that suggest reactions that are not related to a single situation but that are a reflection of your consistent personal beliefs and behaviors.

1. In the past month, when have you asked a colleague for help on a project?

____

____

2. What does it take for you to ask for help? How much discomfort must you experience in order to seek assistance from someone else?

____

____

____

3. Are your tendencies to ask for help similar or different at home and at work?

____

____

4. When you see other people struggling with a task or project, do you offer them help? If yes, how do you do this? If not, why not?

____

____

____

____

____

5. When you are receiving advice from a professional, such as a doctor, dentist, or lawyer, what is your role in the relationship?

____

____

Reciprocity Assessment (continued)

6. When you are receiving advice from a professional at work, such as someone with expertise in technology or finance or an area in which you have no extensive personal experience, what is your role in this relationship?

____

____

7. Think of a specific situation in the past year in which you have received significant assistance from someone at work or at home. How did you feel about this interaction? To what extent did it make you more competent? To what extent did it make you feel less competent? Were you grateful for this assistance? If not, why not?

____

____

____

____

____

____

____

____

8. Consider a situation in which you achieved a significant goal at work or at home. What proportion of that achievement was the result of your personal efforts? If other people helped you in that achievement, describe that person's role and efforts in comparison to your own.

____

____

____

____

____

Reciprocity Assessment (continued)

9. Think of something that you recently learned and then shared with your organization, family, or community. How did you share it? How was your effort to share that information received? How will that influence your next attempt to share information and insights with others?

____

____

____

____

____

____

10. Think of a situation in which you have been personally helped by a colleague in an unexpected way. Perhaps it was from a colleague who was a competitor or a colleague who was from a different part of your organization and had no personal stake in helping you. Since that interaction, how have you reciprocated that colleague's efforts?

____

____

____

____

____

Resilience Assessment

For a computerized administration of this assessment, log on to www.RenewalCoaching.com, then select Assessment.

Date:

Stage of Renewal Coaching

- Not started
- In progress—3 months
- In progress—6 months
- In progress—9 months
- In progress—12 or more months

Instructions: Respond to each of the following statements quickly, providing your first impulse as the answer. A response of 10 is the strongest possible agreement, and 1 is the strongest possible disagreement. There are no correct answers. However, the assessment will be most useful to you if you provide the most authentic response, and that is likely to be the first response that comes to mind.

Statement	Strongly Disagree → Strongly Agree
1. Almost every week, I encounter a situation that is past my breaking point. I don't know if I can bounce back from it.	1 2 3 4 5 6 7 8 9 10
2. When I encounter failure, the causes are almost always factors beyond my control.	1 2 3 4 5 6 7 8 9 10
3. I have recently suffered a professional disappointment, and I doubt I can ever make it up to my boss or my organization.	1 2 3 4 5 6 7 8 9 10
4. I have recently suffered a personal relationship loss, and I probably will not ever have another chance for a similar relationship success.	1 2 3 4 5 6 7 8 9 10
5. If I ask for help from colleagues, they will know that I am incapable of doing adequate work on my own.	1 2 3 4 5 6 7 8 9 10
6. When I encounter silence in a personal relationship, it usually means that the other person is disappointed or angry with me.	1 2 3 4 5 6 7 8 9 10
7. When I think of tragic events in the news or in history, most of them were just unavoidable.	1 2 3 4 5 6 7 8 9 10
8. The significant changes that have happened in my life were usually caused by forces outside my control.	1 2 3 4 5 6 7 8 9 10

Resilience Assessment (continued)

Statement	Strongly Disagree → Strongly Agree
9. In the past year, I have attempted to make a major personal change, but outside influences prevented me from following through on the change.	1 2 3 4 5 6 7 8 9 10
10. In the past year, I have attempted to make an important professional or educational change, but I could not get the support from organizations and institutions to make it work.	1 2 3 4 5 6 7 8 9 10

Total score: ________

0–25	You are an amazingly resilient person. When you encounter disappointments, you bounce back, confident in your ability to learn from the experience and almost certain that you can influence the results the next time. This strong confidence in your ability and healthy skepticism of the influences of the outside world will generally serve you well. However, others may sometimes see your confidence as cockiness or arrogance. Your confidence in the superiority of your influence on the world can also appear to be indifference to the forces of nature and society. You may also underestimate powerful social forces that should sometimes be taken more seriously.
26–50	You are a moderately resilient person, fairly confident in your abilities to withstand the slings and arrows of outrageous fortune, or at least of daily life. Your amiability and self-confidence are balanced by a healthy understanding of outside influences on your personal and professional success. Your equanimity, however, can be interpreted by others as being a bit wishy-washy or inconsistent, so you will benefit from clarifying your analysis of situations. For example, when you encounter a disappointment, it will be helpful if you articulate clearly where your personal responsibility begins and the impact of outside forces ends.
51–75	You will benefit from an explicit focus on improving your personal resilience. Your life experiences have influenced your thought patterns in a troubling way, robbing you of confidence in your own abilities to influence your future. This can create a sense of fatalism that becomes a self-fulfilling prophesy. If you think things cannot improve, then they probably will not. If you believe that your influence on events around you is limited, then you will probably be correct. You would benefit from focusing on some very short-term (one to four day) objectives in which you can demonstrate your ability to influence your own life and have an impact on events around you. Rather than pursue an overwhelmingly large objective and risk disappointment, consider the pursuit of a series of small victories. The cumulative effect of them might surprise you.

Resilience Assessment (continued)

76–100 You have suffered serious personal and professional setbacks, and because you are convinced that these disappointments are beyond your control, you are heading toward a future of despair unless you take serious and immediate corrective action. Your support structure at home and at work may have abandoned you as your cloud of bleak disappointment tends to scare away those who might try to offer assistance. While you may think that you are simply being open and honest about the way the world is, your views can strike others as bleak and foreboding, and therefore even people who care about you do not spend much time around you. That makes for a very lonely and disappointing life, which worsens the cycle of solitude, anger, and cynicism in which you find yourself. Fortunately, there are skills you can develop that will lead to resilience and renewal, but this will require some intense focus and concentration on a daily, even an hourly, basis. You will need to check your thought patterns for accuracy and engage in resilience exercises that will allow you to demonstrate your impact on your life and on the world around you. You deserve to have a much happier life than you have right now.

Open Response Assessment

Complete each of these open-ended questions, being attentive to trends and patterns that suggest reactions that are not related to a single situation but that are a reflection of your consistent personal beliefs and behaviors.

1. Think of a time that you would describe yourself as resilient. What happened, and why is that evidence of resilience? Would other people who know you well answer this question the same way? Why or why not?

____

____

____

____

____

____

Resilience Assessment (continued)

2. List the losses in your life on a time line divided into decades. Describe what you remember doing in the weeks immediately following the loss. Then, describe the actions you took over the next six months. What patterns do you notice about how you respond to loss?

3. Think of an incident where you were less resilient. What seems to be different about the incidents where you are less resilient?

4. How does your behavior change as a result of medication, alcohol, or exercise? When you have endured a loss, how has it affected your personal and work relationships? What other elements of your daily routines have been affected by the experience of loss?

Resilience Assessment (continued)

5. List the events in your life that you consider to be successful or even pinnacle experiences. What losses preceded these positive events?

____

____

____

____

6. What do you believe about the relationship between positive events and losses? If you detect an association between the positive and negative, explore that. Which events come first? How does one event lead to the next?

____

____

____

____

____

7. Are you more resilient when you experience loss in certain areas of your life over others? For example, are you more resilient with financial loss than relationship loss? Loss of relationships rather than physical health?

____

____

____

8. Bring to mind a recent loss from which you have recovered. What strategies were successful?

____

____

____

____

Resilience Assessment (continued)

9. Think of one or two people you would regard as resilient. List what you know to be the strategies they use to respond to loss. Are any of the strategies you use to bounce back from loss similar to theirs?

10. What undermines your ability to be resilient? Do you isolate yourself during times of trouble? Do you procrastinate in your work? Do you doubt your gifts and abilities? What do you need to learn about resiliency in order to become more resilient?

11. How does your organization and family respond to loss, challenges, and change? How have these responses influenced you?

Resonance Assessment

For a computerized administration of this assessment, log on to www.RenewalCoaching.com, then select Assessment.

Date:

Stage of Renewal Coaching

- Not started
- In progress—3 months
- In progress—6 months
- In progress—9 months
- In progress—12 or more months

Instructions: Respond to each of the following statements quickly, providing your first impulse as the answer. A response of 10 is the strongest possible agreement, and 1 is the strongest possible disagreement. There are no correct answers. However, the assessment will be most useful to you if you provide the most authentic response, and that is likely to be the first response that comes to mind.

Statement	**Strongly Disagree → Strongly Agree**
1. When I saw a colleague I didn't know well or a complete stranger crying, I thought, "Get a grip!" It really made me uncomfortable, and the last thing I wanted to know was the details of this person's life. They may have a problem, but it certainly doesn't involve me.	1 2 3 4 5 6 7 8 9 10
2. Whenever I see a group of people laughing, it makes me worry that either I didn't get the joke or perhaps that they are secretly laughing at me. I never join in the laughter but either avoid the situation entirely or suggest that we've got serious work to do and we had better get to it.	1 2 3 4 5 6 7 8 9 10
3. When I notice a friend, family member, or colleague who is clearly fearful, I try to help them snap out of it. "Hey," I tell them, "you're not a kid, and there are no dragons under the bed anymore!" If they pull this fear act too often, I tell them to grow up and start acting their age. In fact, it's embarrassing to me when people around me show fear.	1 2 3 4 5 6 7 8 9 10
4. When I see someone taking pride in something minuscule, I think it's sort of stupid, like thinking that their grandkid is the only cute baby in the world or their dog's doing a trick is somehow indicative of the intellect of the owner. "Okay. Your kid's on the honor roll and is really, really gifted—and so are you. So can we get back to work now?"	1 2 3 4 5 6 7 8 9 10

Resonance Assessment (continued)

Statement	Strongly Disagree → Strongly Agree
5. When colleagues or friends are perpetually happy, I wonder what sort of drugs they are taking. These are serious times, and serious people don't get into good moods unless they are in active denial. They must not watch the news, and they certainly don't know what's going on in our organization, or they would be a bit more sober and take life more seriously. Their good moods make me question their judgment and grip on reality.	1 2 3 4 5 6 7 8 9 10
6. I really admire a couple of our senior leaders—the ones whom other people seem to despise. They are tough but fair, real Attila the Hun types, taking no prisoners. When they chew somebody out publicly, it's sort of fun to watch, because they say out loud what I think—what everybody thinks.	1 2 3 4 5 6 7 8 9 10
7. My siblings, family, and close friends know not to intrude too much on my personal feelings. I'm a loner, and I don't appreciate anybody else, no matter how close they may be, asking me about how I feel about things.	1 2 3 4 5 6 7 8 9 10
8. I listened to a colleague give a presentation about volunteer work and public service, and he started choking up at the end when he was talking about how important it was to him. It was humiliating and embarrassing and totally unprofessional.	1 2 3 4 5 6 7 8 9 10
9. If I see a colleague or friend get too emotional, I try to help them out by lightening up the mood and changing the subject.	1 2 3 4 5 6 7 8 9 10
10. It hardly ever happens, but on those very rare occasions when my emotions get the better of me, I just excuse myself. I'd much rather be alone than around family, friends, or colleagues when I'm emotional.	1 2 3 4 5 6 7 8 9 10

Total score: ________

Resonance Assessment (continued)

10–40	You resonate with others so much that you wear your emotions on your sleeve and you support others who do the same. It is possible, however, that when you think about the term *emotional intelligence,* you give the first part of the term disproportionate weight compared to the latter. While sharing your emotions is fine, you need not share them with everyone and in every situation. Although you are a wonderfully empathetic person, not everyone else around you shares that gift, and you might benefit from being a bit more judicious before letting loose your next emotional outburst or encouraging a colleague to do the same. Have you noticed that you are spending a great deal of time dealing with the most intimate and personal problems of your colleagues when you needed to get a project finished? You are a thoughtful, caring soul, and the world needs people like you. But the world also needs people to get back to work and focus on the task at hand without becoming overwhelmed by the emotions of others. There are, unfortunately, people in the world with very destructive emotions—anger, jealousy, hate—and you are vulnerable to being sucked into their emotional vortex if your otherwise wonderful sense of empathy gets out of control.
41–70	You show balanced resonance, sharing your emotions at times and keeping them in check at other times. You are able to support your colleagues, friends, and family when they are in distress without becoming the amateur therapist in the office. While the more hardbitten and cynical colleagues in your organization turn a blind eye to the needs of others, you seem to know when it is appropriate to laugh with those who laugh and weep with those who weep. You are able to give the benefit of the doubt to those in distress without being taken advantage of by someone who uses emotional displays for the purpose of manipulation. Your equanimity allows you to coach your colleagues who are too cold and rational to be more sensitive, and to help others who bring a daily dose of drama to the office to focus on the world around them. You've probably been burned a few times at both extremes, spending too much time with the melodramatic relative, friend, or colleague, but all things considered, you've decided that is a better way to live than failing to be there when people needed you.
71–100	It's almost always good to be rational—and you certainly are. It's sometimes good to be alone—and you probably are. But it's not good to be angry, sullen, cynical, distrustful, vengeful, spiteful, and full of regret—and chances are you have been all of those at some time in the past few weeks. Your world is full of people attempting to take advantage of you, manipulate you, and prey on your feelings had those feelings not long ago been securely placed in a deep freezer. Perhaps something happened—a rejection by a parent,

Resonance Assessment (continued)

lover, best friend, or boss—and it seems like yesterday when the words "this isn't working out" or "I'm leaving" or, perhaps worst of all, there was a sudden absence accompanied by no words at all. So you have filled in that silence with the worst possible scenario. Perhaps it is beginning to occur to you that rationality alone is not the key to happiness. Lots of people know that the square of the hypotenuse is equal to the sum of the square of the two sides and they are right—but being right is not enough. They may also "know" about their judgments of their friends, relatives, in-laws, and colleagues, and perhaps they are right as well. But a life of unending judgment of others is ultimately a life of solitude and misery. Many people do not learn this until long after their careers and relationships have taken a downward spiral. We hope that you will work on resonance not because anyone else deserves a better opinion from you, but because you deserve to be less miserable than you are right now.

Open Response Assessment

Complete each of these open-ended questions, being attentive to trends and patterns that suggest reactions that are not related to a single situation but that are a reflection of your consistent personal beliefs and behaviors.

1. When you are in a difficult or unpleasant situation, do you maintain your presence, or do you either disengage and shut down or become overly aggressive for the situation?

____

____

2. What do you add to meetings or gatherings? How would others answer this question about you?

____

____

____

____

Resonance Assessment (continued)

3. What makes you dissonant? What impact does it have on others when you are fearful, angry, without hope or faith?

____

____

____

____

4. What does it take for you to pull yourself out of a dissonant funk? Once you decide to become more resonant, how long does it take you to do so?

____

____

____

____

5. How do you know when you are headed toward a dissonant state of mind? What patterns are present in the hours preceding this?

____

____

____

____

6. Who do you know who is really great to be with? Why exactly is that? What does this person do? What does he or she say? What does his or her presence do for you? Do you think differently or feel differently around this person?

____

____

____

____

____

____

Resonance Assessment (continued)

7. What emotions describe your family, organization, or work team? How many would you say are positive, such as *happy, optimistic, excited, creative, kind,* and *generous?* How many would you say are negative, such as *fearful, depressed, lonely, secretive, jealous, or miserly?*

8. Who in your own life would benefit from a compassionate perspective? Who empathizes with you but also has constructive input for you to think about? Who needs your compassionate perspective?

Relationship Assessment

For a computerized administration of this assessment, log on to www.RenewalCoaching.com, then select Assessment.

Date:

Stage of Renewal Coaching

- Not started
- In progress—3 months
- In progress—6 months
- In progress—9 months
- In progress—12 or more months

Instructions: Respond to each of the following statements quickly, providing your first impulse as the answer. A response of 10 is the strongest possible agreement, and 1 is the strongest possible disagreement. There are no correct answers. However, the assessment will be most useful to you if you provide the most authentic response, and that is likely to be the first response that comes to mind.

Statement	**Strongly Disagree → Strongly Agree**
1. I have at least one close personal relationship where it is safe to be who I am, without any acting or pretending.	1 2 3 4 5 6 7 8 9 10
2. In my professional life, I have at least one relationship in which I can accept negative feedback without any threat to the relationship.	1 2 3 4 5 6 7 8 9 10
3. I can be very hurt by or disappointed with someone close to me, forgive him or her, and still maintain a close relationship.	1 2 3 4 5 6 7 8 9 10
4. When I hear other people speak with contempt about someone close to them, it makes me very uncomfortable.	1 2 3 4 5 6 7 8 9 10
5. When I feel like a failure, I know someone I can talk with about this who will not judge me as a failure.	1 2 3 4 5 6 7 8 9 10
6. I can recall a conversation within the past couple of weeks in which I simply listened to the other person without interruption.	1 2 3 4 5 6 7 8 9 10

Relationship Assessment (continued)

Statement	Strongly Disagree → Strongly Agree
7. My closest colleagues at work know that they can occasionally blow off steam with me and that I will forgive them, even if they are a little bit out of control.	1 2 3 4 5 6 7 8 9 10
8. Some of my closest relationships are with people who give me candid advice, even when their candor hurts a little bit.	1 2 3 4 5 6 7 8 9 10
9. I can almost always think of something encouraging and nice to say to other people.	1 2 3 4 5 6 7 8 9 10
10. I have personally expressed gratitude to a person close to me at least once in the past week.	1 2 3 4 5 6 7 8 9 10

Total score: ________

10–40	You claim to embrace a rugged individualism, but the reality is that yours is a sad, lonely, and difficult life. People are stupid and corrupt, and they disappoint you at every turn. Sometimes you'd like to confide in someone, but if you took that risk, your spouse or lover would leave you, your friends would make fun of you, and your colleagues at work would use it against you. So you never risk being authentic. When you watch movies in which the heroic rugged individualist blows away the vile enemy, you get an emotional rush that flesh and blood humans have never provided for you. Because both the Terminator and Bat Girl are otherwise engaged, you are very likely to leave the theater alone.
41–70	You are nobody's fool. Several times you have given friends and colleagues the benefit of the doubt, and you've been burned. You tried to be supportive, accepting, and nonjudgmental, but it's tiresome after a while. It feels as if you're the only one doing the work in these relationships, and it's just not fair that you bear the burden of sustaining them. When it comes to new relationships at work and in your personal life, you're really on the fence. Perhaps you will give people the benefit of the doubt and listen to them, accept them, and appreciate them. Perhaps. But if you hit the wall again with their disappointment, disloyalty, and disrespect, then you're ready to smack them down, at least verbally, and cut them off emotionally.
71–100	You may not have a great many friends, but you are very fortunate to have a few people in your personal and professional life who are true friends. You can confide in them and they in you. You attract these people because you too are a true friend, giving time, acceptance, and gratitude to others. If you scored in the 90s, then you are living by the Platinum Rule, giving more to others than you expect them to give to you.

Relationship Assessment (continued)

Open Response Assessment

Complete each of these open-ended questions, being attentive to trends and patterns that suggest reactions that are not related to a single situation but that are a reflection of your consistent personal beliefs and behaviors.

1. Think about the ten most important people in your life. How often do you initiate resonant interactions with them?

2. What do you have to give to others? Do you have expertise and knowledge about something that someone else needs? Who needs your talents?

3. Who needs you to listen to them as they process something important or troublesome in their life or work? What do you wish someone would listen to you about?

4. What do you need to learn or have that would allow you to accomplish something that matters? Who can you ask for help with this?

Relationship Assessment (continued)

5. Whom do you need to thank for what they have given you or taught to you or shown to you through their example? Thank five people every day, and when you do, tell them specifically what you are grateful for: "When you showed me how you set up the time line for that project, I had a breakthrough on the project I am working on. Thank you for sharing your expertise with me."

____

____

____

6. Have you lost important relationships in your life with a colleague or family member? How did it happen? And have you repaired an important relationship in your life? What actions did you take to do this?

____

____

____

____

____

7. What do you love about the work you do? What specifically do you love about the tasks, the processes, and the relationships involved in your work?

____

____

____

____

8. Who inspires you? Whom do you inspire? Who would love for you to notice him or her and what would that allow this person to do? How would he or she think differently about themselves?

____

____

____

____

____

Relationship Assessment (continued)

9. How diligent are you at meeting your obligations and commitments to others? Do you follow through on promises? Do others consider you trustworthy? Can you be counted on?

10. Who loves you, and whom do you love? What does this tell you about yourself? Try to describe in words what you mean to others. Now try to describe in words what others mean to you. What does the difference between these two descriptions suggest to you about your relationships?

Renewal Assessment

For a computerized administration of this assessment, log on to www.RenewalCoaching.com, then select Assessment.

Date:

Stage of Renewal Coaching

- Not started
- In progress—3 months
- In progress—6 months
- In progress—9 months
- In progress—12 or more months

Instructions: Respond to each of the following statements quickly, providing your first impulse as the answer. A response of 10 is the strongest possible agreement, and 1 is the strongest possible disagreement. There are no correct answers. However, the assessment will be most useful to you if you provide the most authentic response, and that is likely to be the first response that comes to mind.

Statement	**Strongly Disagree → Strongly Agree**
1. Even if I'm meeting my usual goals and being very efficient on my job, I'm not completely fulfilled unless I am achieving a higher purpose serving the greater good.	1 2 3 4 5 6 7 8 9 10
2. I can think of several times when, after undergoing adversity, I'm actually better off after the adversity than I was before it.	1 2 3 4 5 6 7 8 9 10
3. I can identify very specifically the source of my greatest inspiration.	1 2 3 4 5 6 7 8 9 10
4. When I need physical renewal, I know of specific and consistent activities and routines that will be helpful for me.	1 2 3 4 5 6 7 8 9 10
5. I am very aware of when I need renewal and I know the warning signs that suggest to me that I need support and renewal.	1 2 3 4 5 6 7 8 9 10
6. I am able to reflect on my past and think about mistakes I have made without being obsessed and overwhelmed by them. I know my "lessons learned" and can apply them to my daily life.	1 2 3 4 5 6 7 8 9 10

Renewal Assessment (continued)

Statement	Strongly Disagree → Strongly Agree
7. I have forgiven myself for my past mistakes.	1 2 3 4 5 6 7 8 9 10
8. When I need emotional renewal, I know of people and practices that help me gain renewal.	1 2 3 4 5 6 7 8 9 10
9. I have forgiven others, even those who have hurt me very deeply.	1 2 3 4 5 6 7 8 9 10
10. I can think of a specific example when I have helped to provide renewal to a colleague or a loved one within the past week.	1 2 3 4 5 6 7 8 9 10

Total score: ________

10–40	You are so emotionally and physically exhausted it's amazing that you have the energy to read this—but because you also can't get a decent night's sleep, perhaps you hope that this book will help cure your insomnia. The physical, emotional, and mental challenges all run together. Your sleep disruption might be related to your eating habits, alternatively too much and too little food. When you feel either famished or stuffed, then physical renewal—or for that matter even a walk around the block—can feel like an insurmountable challenge. Most of all, you are very alone. You can be in a crowd in Times Square, among family and friends who care about you, or lying on your couch into the tenth hour of a television and ice cream marathon—it doesn't matter. It's all the same feeling of isolation and despair. You've made some mistakes—some real whoppers, in fact. But the punishment you have already received from others for those mistakes is never enough, so you continue to berate yourself, accuse yourself, and administer punishment that far outweighs the crime. Although you know, on an intellectual level, how irrational this is, you can't seem to shake it. Whatever your accomplishments and successes, the liabilities always outweigh the assets on your emotional balance sheet, leaving you in a chronic state of psychological deficit. You need a break—in every sense of the word—and the sooner you make the break from this landscape of disease, the sooner you will begin the road to renewal.

Renewal Assessment (continued)

41–70	Although you occasionally find new energy, it sometimes feels as if you are treading water in the middle of a vast ocean and there isn't much for you to hang on to when the waves crash around you. Perhaps the most disconcerting statement that others make is the claim that "you've got it all" when they refer to your successes at work or your apparently happy personal life. But there are days when the successes on which other people focus offer little or no fulfillment. Promotions and raises come and go and you accept congratulations with little real enthusiasm. When your friends and colleagues express envy of you, you are thinking, "If you only knew how little this means to me." There are exceptions, of course, as you consider moments of physical, emotional, and mental renewal in the past. You sometimes think about re-creating those moments, but transforming thought into action is inconsistent and distant.
71–100	You have found the sources of renewal in your life and you regularly use them. Although you can certainly be effective in your professional life and you are capable of maintaining and sustaining meaningful personal relationships, you find true meaning in service and a contribution to the greater good. You are not superhuman, but you seem to have a level of calm and equanimity that allows you to keep your cool when other people around you are panicking. You have faced disappointment and loss, and you endure not through blind stoicism but through renewal. When your body and spirit is down, you show the wisdom to stop, rest, and restore yourself, meeting your mental, physical, and spiritual needs. As successful as you are, you are the first to acknowledge that you have not achieved this success alone. You are regularly aware of the role that other people—today and in history—have played in your success. Though you rarely claim credit for it, your personal example serves as sources of renewal for other people.

Open Response Assessment

Complete each of these open-ended questions, being attentive to trends and patterns that suggest reactions that are not related to a single situation but are a reflection of your consistent personal beliefs and behaviors.

1. What do you have a second chance at right now in your life? Something that has previously been hard for you but that you can choose right this moment to look at through the lens of possibility?

___

___

___

Renewal Assessment (continued)

2. What have you been resisting? Is there a problem or reality you did not expect and do not desire but that you have to respond to nevertheless? What would it take for you to respond to it as a welcomed opportunity instead of a problem to solve?

3. What do you need to do for yourself each day in order to feel energized? For one week, record in a journal what you did to renew each day and what that allowed you to accomplish or feel about what you do in your work or with your family.

4. What do you need to do for others in your work and family in order to feel energized? What does this allow them to accomplish? What does giving of yourself this way allow them to accomplish?

Renewal Assessment (continued)

5. What are your boundless, most idealistic dreams for what you wish to do for others and the world? What is your legacy?

___

___

___

6. Have you taken remarkable actions in your life already that others would say have created something good for others? What did it take for you to do that?

___

___

___

7. What are you so passionate about that you wake up in the morning thinking about it and can't wait to get out of bed?

___

8. What has happened in your life that at the time seemed like the worst possible thing that could have happened but now you would say is one of the best things you went through because of what happened afterward? What *did* happen afterward?

___

___

___

9. What has this "worst possible thing" allowed you to do now? What were the lessons that you are grateful for?

___

___

___

Renewal Assessment (continued)

10. What adversity from your past are you still in pain from? Why can't you let go of it? What does hanging on to this adversity rob you of in the present? Have you been sheltering yourself from taking risks because you don't want to experience loss, pain, or adversity? What legacy are you giving up on because it feels safer to think small?

CHAPTER 5

Interpreting Assessment Results

If you completed the assessments in the previous chapter, you may be bewildered. Where am I? What are my real strengths? Some assessments suggest I'm brilliant and others suggest—in the nicest possible way, of course—I'm clueless. Others leave me in the very uncomfortable and ambiguous position of not knowing if I have a strength or a weakness. If you have any of these feelings, then the assessments have offered you a glimpse into wisdom, described by Merriam and Caffarella (1999) as the pinnacle of adult thought. One reason that wisdom is difficult to describe accurately, however, is that the characteristics of wisdom can be in tension with one another. As Figure 5.1 illustrates, some feedback from your Renewal Coaching assessments describes your abilities in insight and analysis; other assessments focus on empathy and intuition. We can all think of people who are, for example, exceptionally strong analysts. They have the uncanny ability to identify our faults, and the blissful social ignorance to tell us all about them. These are people who may be smart but certainly are not wise. Others may have the empathy and intuition of a mystic, yet their optimism and hope can seem misplaced when they allow their faith to supplant the facts. Regardless of how sympathetic these people may be, they are endearing but not wise.

Therefore, these assessments suggest not a "final examination" that you have completed but rather only preliminary feedback on your journey toward renewal. One characteristic of the assessments that you have already

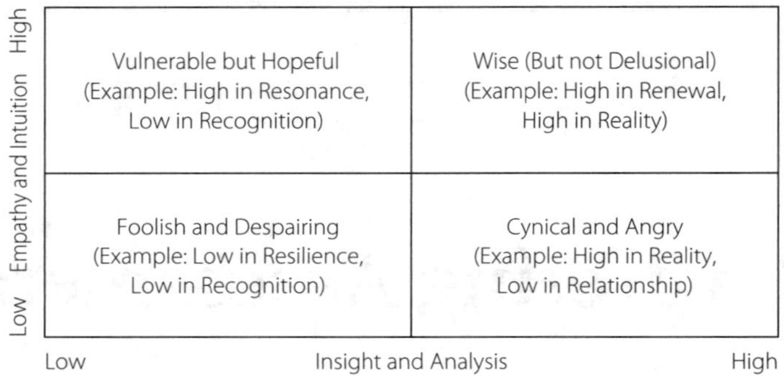

Figure 5.1 Renewal Assessment in Perspective

discovered is that a "high" score is not always good. The opposite of gullibility, for example, is not necessarily nuanced thought and deep wisdom but may be an unbearable cynicism and distrust. As you consider your assessment results, ask which results are similar to each other and which are different. High scores in one area do not necessarily lead to high scores in other areas. The horizontal axis in Figure 5.1 represents learning and factual observations; the vertical axis represents insight and emotional intelligence.

INSIGHT AND INTUITION: FINDING THE GOLDEN MEAN

When applying the results of the Renewal Coaching assessments, high scores in reality, recognition, and reciprocity represent strengths on the horizontal axis and are often associated with analytical insight. However, it is not possible to "think your way to wisdom." Great analysts can be deeply angry and cynical people. The vertical axis is associated with strengths in resonance, resilience, relationship, and renewal. These strengths, however formidable, are not sufficient without insight.

Review your own assessment results and consider which quadrant best describes you.

If any assessment has value, its purpose is not merely to provide a label but rather to suggest constructive actions. The good news is that the preponderance of research evidence suggests that individuals and organizations can change in deep, profound, and lasting ways. The bad news is that these changes will require, first, the confrontation of the fact that we are far from the ideal of wisdom now and, second, a commitment to actions that will be challenging and counterintuitive. In fact, the sheer number of action steps suggested by your assessments may be overwhelming, and that is what we address in the next part of this chapter.

SETTING PRIORITIES

This chapter has thus far focused on the results of your Renewal Coaching assessments. Not surprisingly, you have probably generated a long—perhaps overwhelming—list of actions that all appear to be priorities. A decision analysis matrix, such as the one presented in Figure 5.2, can help you identify how to transform the laundry list of actions into a high-impact action list. By "high-impact" we mean focusing on the action items that meet two criteria: first, they have a high probability of influencing your goals; and second, they can be implemented by decisions that you have the ability to make. The sample matrix in Figure 5.2 illustrates the intersection of these decision criteria, revealing four ways to categorize the actions on your list:

Do it	High impact, high personal authority
Drop it	Low impact, high personal authority
Avoid it	Low impact, low personal authority
Negotiate it	High impact, low personal authority

The assessment results that you have already considered may yield prospective tasks that fall into all four quadrants. Consider, for example, Marie, a senior manager in a Web design company who recently completed the Reality Assessment. Her score of 28 suggests that although she is a nice person—perhaps too nice, she thinks—she is increasingly angry that she has been taken advantage of by colleagues and bosses. The words of the

Impact \ Personal Authority	Low	High
High	High Impact, Low Authority NEGOTIATE IT	High Impact, High Authority DO IT!
Low	Low Impact, Low Authority AVOID IT	Low Impact, High Authority DROP IT

Figure 5.2 Decision Analysis Matrix

assessment include this statement that struck home for Marie: "You may be secretly angry with yourself for being taken advantage of so much in the past, but you continue to accept the statements and behavior of other people without critical analysis." Based on this assessment, Marie and her coach brainstormed the following list of actions. As with any brainstorming process, the contents of this list were generated without judgment or evaluation; they are simply the impulsive responses that Marie and the coach came up with on the basis of the feedback obtained from the assessment.

1. Tell her boss tomorrow that his expectations for the latest Web design project were unreasonable and intrusive, and she wasn't going to meet them.
2. Announce a change in her work schedule to allow her to spend an hour at the gym on the way to work each day.
3. Gather evidence on high-quality projects that are similar to the ones Marie is now working on and create a set of benchmarks to evaluate the complexity and work requirements for her projects.
4. Have a conversation with her boss to consider an analytical framework to link project demands with the time and resources available.
5. Allocate one-third of her work to a coworker.
6. Let the project slide; the only thing that gets anyone's attention around here is a crisis.
7. Get it done; the economy's tough and if she doesn't accede to the unreasonable demands of her boss, some other eager coworker will do it and survive the next round of layoffs but Marie will not.
8. In the next project meeting, list the assumptions that were made by Marie, the team, and her boss, and list the evidence that supported (or failed to support) each of these assumptions.

Marie is just getting warmed up, and by the time she finishes the Renewal Coaching assessments, she will have easily developed scores, perhaps hundreds, of tasks. Such a list will be unfocused and unhelpful, and Marie will be even more frustrated than she was before. The Decision Analysis Matrix will allow Marie to prioritize her actions. Table 5.1 illustrates how Marie analyzed each alternative with regard to its impact and to her personal authority.

Marie's analysis reveals that three of her eight potential actions fall within the Do It! quadrant, with high authority and high impact. Equipped with these insights, she can enjoy the catharsis of her brainstorming session

Table 5.1 Marie's Decision Analysis

Action	Authority	Impact	Do it!	Drop It	Avoid It	Negotiate It
1. Tell the boss to go to blazes	High	Low		X		
2. Change schedule and get healthy	Low	High				X
3. Gather evidence	High	High	X			
4. Discuss analytical framework with boss	High	High	X			
5. Allocate 1/3 workload to coworker	Low	Low			X	
6. Let the project slide and precipitate a crisis	High	Low		X		
7. Get it done and accept the abuse	High	Low		X		
8. Identify assumptions and evidence	High	High	X			

with her coach but not waste time, energy, and emotion on potential actions that will fail to provide impact and for which she has limited authority.

In each of the following chapters you will be asked to consider the same questions that Marie faced:

> What actions are suggested by my assessments? This will be a process of brainstorming many possible actions that you will list without evaluation or judgment.
>
> To what degree will these actions have impact for my most important priorities?
>
> To what degree do I have the ability to control these actions?

Answering these questions will allow you to categorize each potential action under Do It!, Drop It, Avoid It, or Negotiate It.

You will conclude each chapter by focusing on your Do It! list—the actions with the highest impact and in which you have the greatest personal authority. You will also enjoy the immensely therapeutic process of putting into the ash bin those tasks in the Drop It and Avoid It categories. Really: you might want to light a fire and stoke it with these tasks. Get rid of them. Bury them, forget about them. Many important opportunities are awaiting you, if only you will remove from the table those actions that are harmful or irrelevant.

BEFORE THE SEMINAR

If you are using this workbook as part of the Foundations of Renewal Coaching seminar, then please complete all of the pre-seminar assignments in Part One of the Renewal Coaching Workbook. You can use the forms provided in the workbook or the online forms located at www.RenewalCoaching.com. The first thing you will do in the seminar is work on your 100-Day Renewal Project. By completing the decision matrix discussed in this chapter, along with the other pre-seminar work offered in Part One, you will be able to make the best use of your time in the seminar.

If you are using this workbook for independent work, you are now ready to proceed. You will begin with your 100-Day Renewal Project, then explore each element of Renewal Coaching. In Part Three: Reflection, you will identify specific ways to apply what you have learned about Renewal Coaching to your personal and professional goals. In Part Four: Sustaining, you will learn how to measure your success and, most important, explore how you contribute to the greater good. The key to sustainability is not merely efficiency and effectiveness, but finding meaning in life that extends beyond yourself and your organization.

CHAPTER 6

Your 100-Day Renewal Project

In this chapter you will consider the 100-Day Renewal Project from the perspective of your world at work, at home, or in your community. Whether you are a coach, client, or coaching leader, you can use this technique to accomplish the short-term wins that are a vital element of sustainable change. In this project, you will carry out specific actions that lead to the achievement of personal and organizational goals that consider the greater good and that are meaningful to you. At the same time, you will use the results from your seven Renewal Coaching assessments to determine specific actions you can take to develop a culture and climate necessary to renewal.

Before we explain what the 100-Day Renewal Project is, we want to clarify what it is not. It is not a strategic plan, a Gantt chart, or even an action plan, although these documents may be important to the success of your organization. The 100-Day Renewal Project is a container in which leaders, teams, coaches, and clients can plan the high-powered actions that will jump-start the important changes needed within the context of the project you have selected to develop a culture that supports renewal. It is the primary tool that Renewal Coaches and leaders will use in every coaching conversation.

The 100-Day Renewal Project ensures the following:

- High-powered action to create a climate of renewal
- Mindful application of the seven Renewal Coaching assessments

- Responsibility for the client leader
- Accountability for actions taken
- A record of what action was taken
- Reflection on the results and impact of actions taken
- Intense focus on the advancement of the project

ONE HUNDRED DAYS?

Ever since American President Franklin Roosevelt used his first hundred days in office to take deliberate action to fight the Great Depression and bring hope to America, people all over the world have understood that there is something special about the first hundred days of any significant change initiative. It is essential that you are clear about what you want to achieve and then that you take immediate and purposeful action every day to make it happen. If you are in the habit of writing up your personal resolutions each New Year's Eve, you already understand the value of purposeful planning and action. What do you feel when you write down a goal? Do you feel optimistic and energized, or are you flooded with anxiety and dread? Your answer probably depends on your personal history of goal setting and goal achieving. It is one thing to set a goal, but it is quite another to achieve it, or even to take the first steps. But if you have experienced the exhilaration of setting a meaningful goal for yourself and actually accomplishing it, then you already have some insight into what it takes to change reality.

If you still doubt the power of a hundred days, consider these examples from history from Sheryl Nance-Nash (2009):

> In February 2005, YouTube inventors Steve Chen, Chad Hurley, and Jawed Karim began developing the website out of a garage in Menlo Park, California. Less than three months later, the first version of the video-sharing site was launched....
>
> In just 116 days, the [delegates to the Constitutional convention] wrote and signed the Constitution that we have now followed for 221 years....
>
> In a little over 100 days (111 to be exact) [Charlie Engle, Ray Zahab, and Kevin Lin] ran more than 4,300 miles, crossing the entire Sahara desert and six countries....
>
> In less than three months in the spring of 1939, Igor Sikorsky designed the first modern-day helicopter, with a single main rotor and tail rotor setup. On September 14, he piloted the new aircraft on its first flight.

What we ask you to embrace now is the fact that the ultimate success of your project and the creation of a climate of renewal depend in large part on what you do in the first hundred days. Your 100-Day Renewal Project will push you to take immediate action to create the future you desire for yourself and your organization. Vision and immediate action are the two hallmarks of goals achieved.

One Hundred Days

What is your personal theory about why the first hundred days matter so much when starting or revitalizing a change? After you write your ideas here, read the next section and then return to this section to add new insights or confirm what you were already thinking.

My personal theory about why the first hundred days matter:

____

____

____

____

____

____

____

My reflections after I read the next section:

____

____

____

WHAT'S THE BIG DEAL ABOUT THE FIRST HUNDRED DAYS?

An inspiring example of the power of the first hundred days of a change initiative comes to us from a council in an urban housing project. From February 1 to May 11 of 2007, the council launched a project called

"100 Days of Change" to improve conditions for residents of the public housing within the project. They began with the broad vision to make the project "the best" by making the homes and neighborhoods great places to live, where "good, quality services are provided right the first time." The strategies the council selected to implement included these four: (1) change the way they carry out repairs, (2) refurbish communal areas, (3) rev up the investment program, and (4) respond to tenants' and leaseholders' issues and concerns. Within each of these strategies, the council and employees took very specific actions, which they documented day by day for each of the first one hundred days.

What the council accomplished is truly remarkable and far exceeds the space we have here in this workbook, but here are a few examples: they reduced call response time to customers needing repairs from over two minutes to thirty-seven seconds, cleaned and repaired all common areas, put in playgrounds and field sports areas, changed budget allocations to focus on these interventions for the next ten years, cut red tape and put decision making in the hands of the housing staff, secured a grant for homes for the elderly, brought in the book mobile, created an online repair request process, sought out tenants who were behind on rent and helped them find solutions, and established street leader and youth groups.

The "100 Days of Change" project shows just what can happen when people come together for a greater good. Yes, they achieved remarkable milestones—even exceeding some of the targets they set for themselves—but more important, they now have the knowledge and experience of what it took to cause these changes. They established patterns, processes, policies, habits, and structures within their organization that support a climate and culture of renewal. This experience gives them confidence to sustain the changes that have occurred, refine processes that need attention, and replicate strategies that make a big difference.

Most one-hundred-day literature is directed at leaders assuming senior positions in businesses and organizations. We agree that leaders who are new to an organization have a small window of time to establish the tenor of their service, and we support the premise that new leaders must have a deliberate plan for setting and communicating their vision, securing early wins, and building networks and inspiring people to action. In fact, we like the idea so much that we extended it to apply to the start of any new initiative. After all, today is the first day of the first hundred days of the rest of your life! If there is a project you need to begin that would make a significant impact on your organization, today is as good a day as any to begin it.

The characteristics of the first one hundred days of any change initiative are briefly described in the following paragraphs.

Momentum

Fresh initiatives have a built-in aura of hope and most initiators of change begin the process with an image in their mind's eye of something better. This vision is compelling. It draws people forward with energy, optimism, and a sense of possibility—essential attitudes for leaders of change who, after they share their vision with others, will inevitably face mild to moderate to strong resistance to the initiative from otherwise very reasonable people. Every leader has a story about how resistance successfully capsized a strong, relevant, innovative, and research-based initiative. Talk about taking the wind out of your sails.

Nudging an initiative that is safely under way in the first hundred days of its conception is not so difficult when you understand that people tend to push back on initiatives they cannot see in the present or picture in their imagination. The thoughtful actions taken in the first hundred days make the desired outcomes visible by creating small wins in the present and illuminating a better future. The potent combination of these two elements at the start of a project creates momentum that is difficult or even impossible to stop.

Trust

Although most people love achieving goals, they also care deeply about the processes used to achieve those goals. Even the greater good is seen as an ill-gotten gain if it comes at the expense of a positive climate in which mistakes are considered opportunities to learn and wins are celebrated. During the first hundred days of any change initiative, leaders have a small amount of time in which to set the tone not only for how it will feel to achieve the outcomes of the project, including a greater good, but also for how the people involved will feel during the process.

Except perhaps in the most punitive and toxic systems, most leaders also have a window at the start of an initiative to earn the trust of the people involved. They do this by communicating clearly, by involving a broad base of people from the beginning, by not being afraid to look objectively at data, and by engaging in thoughtful actions to move the initiative forward.

Leadership

In the first hundred days of any project, change leaders have the opportunity to build and demonstrate credibility. Astoundingly, most leaders appear unaware that there even exists a systematic approach for getting something that matters off the ground (Daly & Watkins, 2006); this ignorance jeopardizes leaders' credibility right from the start. Those who are unaware of the available tools (such as 100-Day Renewal Project plans) often quit before the project even gets off the ground. Some leaders are so defeated by previous unrealized initiatives that they don't even tell another soul about the great ideas in their heads. Other leaders blow their credibility immediately by taking unfocused action to push their vision forward but end up creating disruption and confusion instead. Both approaches are disempowering to the leader and leave their colleagues uninspired and spent.

Leaders of sustained change have learned a great little secret: the leadership they demonstrate through the actions they take in the first hundred days builds trust and relationships, and creates the future.

Hope Turns to Certainty

Strong action taken in the first hundred days leads to visible and early wins, and early wins create hope, faith, and even certainty that the vision of the project will be realized.

Within the first hundred days, the leader and team will likely measure the implementation of actions before they measure the effects of those actions. For example, in the case of the housing project, they could measure and celebrate the percentage of common areas cleaned and repaired right from day one. Over time these leaders will see the impact of that action (cleaned and repaired common areas) in long-term effect indicators, such as the percentage of tenants who buy their property. But by measuring and celebrating the short-term wins of daily actions, they don't have to wait five years before they and others see the fruits of the project.

Before you fill out the Work Initiatives worksheet, return to your personal theory about why the first hundred days matter and add notes that reflect any additional insights and questions that have arisen about the power of the first hundred days.

Work Initiatives

Identify several work initiatives you have led within the past three years. Give them titles and list them in the first column of the following table. In the second column, categorize the current status of each initiative. Finally, reflect on the initiatives that are still implemented and list the actions you recall taking in the first hundred days:

Initiative/Project Title	Current status (such as fully implemented and thriving, partially implemented but moving forward, partially implemented but no longer visible, never got off the ground)	Actions you took in the first hundred days to create momentum, trust, leadership, credibility, and hope
1.		
2.		
3.		
4.		

(continued)

Work Initiatives (continued)

What would you do differently now? What approaches and actions would you replicate in the next project?

____

____

____

____

____

____

____

____

YOUR 100-DAY RENEWAL PROJECT

In Chapter Three you identified one or more personal or organizational opportunities for the pursuit of the greater good. The greater good provides the most compelling reason over the long haul for why you and others want to work and live from the perspective of renewal. Although we want to earn money to care for ourselves and our families, we want to meet objectives so that the organization will thrive, and we want to be happy for as many of the eight to twelve hours per day that most of us spend doing our work. But in the effort to sustain meaningful change, working for the greater good infuses even the most mundane steps with significance.

Every compelling 100-Day Renewal Project has at its core a greater good. In the following worksheet you will identify the essential parts of your 100-Day Renewal Project.

The Greater Good

Step 1: Describe the greater good that you identified in Chapter Three.

____

____

____

Step 2: Select and identify an important project that you are about to start or that you need to start that contributes to your commitment to the greater good.

Your project should:

- Go far beyond your to-do list and stretch you and your team beyond what you have accomplished so far. In fact, you may not yet have the skills and resources to do this project yet, but you are thrilled at the thought of gaining them.
- Be in your circle of control. This means that you must be personally responsible for leading the entire project or parts of the project.
- Require the efforts of other people and networks. By meeting this criteria, your project not only has a greater chance of achieving the levels of commitment required for deep implementation (Reeves, 2008) and systemic change, but also is a powerful way to develop the skills, knowledge, and attitudes needed by those involved to sustain momentum over the long haul.
- Define its specific intended outcome, complete with an identifiable end point, to be made visible by new products, performances, and processes.
- Suggest "early wins" along with milestones and indicators to monitor for purposes of accountability, learning, and celebration.

Name and describe your project here:

____

____

____

____

____

____

(continued)

The Greater Good (continued)

____

____

____

____

Step 3: Identify no more than three primary strategies to move the project forward.

Strategies come from the best of what you can learn or develop to break through "business as usual" and create the context for the desired change. Strategies are antidotes specific to your industry or to a need within your industry for what is currently missing and thus blocking the new reality. For example, in the case of the housing council described earlier, the strategies selected to implement were as follows: (1) Change the way we carry out repairs. (2) Refurbish communal areas. (3) Reenergize our investment program. (4) Respond to tenants' and leaseholders' issues and concerns.

What are your primary strategies for moving your project forward within your industry? Brainstorm as many as you can think of here and then identify three that give you the most leverage, that cause you to feel excitement and hope, and that may even take you out of your current comfort zone:

____

____

____

ACTION

A quick check of the online *Encarta World English Dictionary* (2009) offers several definitions of the word "initiative" the second of which is "the first step in a process that, once taken, determines subsequent events." Great change initiatives deserve every chance of full implementation. Leaders who want to do more than dream will take action to make things happen. These actions should be mindful; that is, they are not to be executed willy-nilly, without thought or care.

Certain high-powered actions are critical to the success of your project and you should apply them to the specific details of the first hundred days of any change initiative you lead. Although the order of actions is unique to every project, leaders who carelessly execute their best strategies to accomplish something that matters without considering these actions set up themselves and their organization for failure or at least unnecessary trouble.

Critical Actions to Take in the First Hundred Days

We have found four main categories of action that must be considered by leaders who desire sustainable change. They include actions that lead to *learning*, actions that lead to using *evidence*, actions that acknowledge and address *attitudes* and emotions, and actions that are in fact *decisions*. We call this the LEAD technique:

> What do you or others on the project need to LEARN?
> What EVIDENCE do you need to collect and analyze?
> What ATTITUDES and emotions must be developed?
> What DECISIONS must be made?

Following are some examples of actions in each LEAD category:

L: Learn	Conduct research. Read books and articles. Review industry standards. Read case studies. Join learning teams and professional groups. Find a mentor who has accomplished the same goal. Hold focus groups. Discuss and understand current procedures, processes, and policies. Get the facts. Discover successes and challenges of others who have done this. Visit successful sites.
E: Evidence	Analyze existing data from financial reports, performance indicators, and resource indicators. Create and collect new data. Evaluate self and organization against industry benchmarks. Hold conversations, ask for different perspectives, hold focus groups, conduct surveys, and evaluations. Involve others in analyzing data, making inferences, and drawing conclusions. Establish processes for continual review, communicate findings to others, track important indicators.
A: Attitudes	Share the vision of the greater good. Have significant conversations with people who care. Involve key people early. Seek different opinions and perspectives. Surface hopes and fears. Establish multiple avenues for conversation between groups. Seek out and listen to those who disagree. Find successful examples. Celebrate early wins. Recognize and reward contributors.
D: Decisions	Determine strategies, timelines, membership, outcomes, indicators, early wins to monitor, project monitoring and evaluations, standards to follow, communication schedules, methods, processes, procedures, policy, practices, rewards, consequences.

Actions That Matter for Renewal

To really get things moving along the path of renewal and sustained change, leaders and coaches intentionally apply the four categories of action (LEAD) to each portion of the Renewal Coaching framework.

Specific actions are informed by the results of your personal assessment in each of the seven Renewal Coaching categories, by the nature and demands of the project itself, by the culture of the organization, and by the identified greater good. Table 6.1 shows how the high-powered actions taken by the housing council (described earlier) relate to each of the seven Renewal Coaching elements.

Notice that these actions leverage the essential requirements of each element of the Renewal Coaching framework and the Renewal Coaching model, which concerns itself with the accomplishment of personal and organization goals as well as a greater good—the outcome that gives meaning to both individuals and organizations. In effect, once the LEAD actions are put into motion, they stimulate the relevant aspect of Renewal Coaching and influence the direction of the project toward sustained change, renewal, and the greater good.

Brainstorm Actions for Your Strategies

Although you will become more specific about the actions you will take as you work through Chapters Eight through Fourteen, you probably have some idea already about actions to take for the strategies you identified. Use the following space to capture your thinking. Write down everything that comes to mind for now. You will have multiple opportunities to revise this initial list as you continue the process:

____

____

____

____

____

Table 6.1 Example of Actions Related to the Renewal Coaching Framework

	L: Learn	E: Evidence	A: Attitudes	D: Decisions
Recognition (Finding patterns of toxicity and renewal)	Flowchart what happens from start to finish when a tenant makes a call to the repair center. Communicate findings to the council and tenants.	Hold focus groups with residents in the communities to capture stories about their experience with calls to the repair center.	Identify current behavioral and emotional patterns about employee response to tenant calls for repairs.	Abolish the bureaucratic panels that slow down response to repairs.
Reality (Confronting change killers in work and life)	Research the practices of call centers known for excellent service.	Within the office and on the agency Web site, post the current data about the percentage of calls answered within specific time limits. Set a new goal and track growth.	Establish data walls. Celebrate wins and inquire into the actions that helped and the actions that hindered.	Identify four indicators to monitor weekly.
Reciprocity (Coaching in harmony)	Review the current policy and practice about how vacant homes are filled. Communicate that information succinctly and in multiple formats to tenants and ask them to provide feedback on the practices described.	Graph the relationship between the current strategies and the percentage of vacant homes filled within certain periods.	Communicate the adverse relationship between vacancies and crime in the community. Call for a concerted effort to fill vacancies. Create a recognition program for new tenants and owners.	Initiate the home matching system that helps potential tenants and owners find the right vacant home and assists them in moving into the space to fill the vacancy within two weeks.
Resilience (Coaching through pain)	Find out the stories of long-term residences of the borough. Record them professionally and upload them to the library system.	Ask what tenants like best about living in the borough and ask what they want more of and less of that would make this community the best.	Showcase the success stories of tenants and neighborhood groups who have shown generosity to newcomers or helped a neighbor in need.	Decide which strategies and actions should be scaled up and which ones should be eliminated.

(continued)

Table 6.1 *(continued)*

	L: Learn	E: Evidence	A: Attitudes	D: Decisions
Relationship (Nurturing the personal elements of coaching)	Learn how the various law enforcement groups currently work together (or don't) to protect the borough from crime and antisocial behavior.	Establish and communicate criteria for team members on this project. Ask each team member to develop a personal learning plan to fully contribute.	Ask the tenants how they feel about the new doors. Support their need to choose a door with a "cat flap" in it if they have a cat in the family.	Establish the youth leadership program in conjunction with the local police academy.
Resonance (Coaching with emotional intelligence)	Provide the team with professional development in "listening."	Interview clients and repair team members to capture the elements of the "best stories" of a complete repair cycle.	Establish monthly interdisciplinary walkabouts to learn firsthand the concerns and issues of the tenants.	Communicate to tenants who are worried about paying the rent all of their options for staying in their home and establishing financial security.
Renewal (Creating energy, meaning, and freedom to sustain the journey)	Establish the artist youth program to teach mosaic art to the children of the community and install multiple community art projects.	Establish and schedule quarterly on-site focus groups with residents for the next ten years. Combine these groups with a weekend festival and celebration of the community. Post data about important indicators such as safety, common space, repair time, and vacancies.	Install and maintain the first in the first-in-the-nation fleet of green eco-repair vehicles to ensure rapid response to tenant needs. Take care of the needs of the fleet personnel and find out what could make the program even better.	Secure funds through the budget and grants to build eco-green housing in conjunction with the new retail and commercial centers.

PULLING YOUR PLAN TOGETHER

At this point you have most of the necessary ingredients to assemble a decent 100-Day Renewal Project. As you work through Chapters Eight through Fourteen in this workbook, or while you are participating in a Renewal Coaching workshop, you will return to your 100-Day Renewal Project plan and add new actions, until finally you have a project ready for implementation. This next section provides the final tools to pull all of the pieces together, with the addition of a timeline and identification of people and networks with whom to work. These two additional ingredients provide cohesion between the actions and create a healthy and necessary sense of urgency.

Timeline

As you progress through this workbook you will accumulate specific actions for your project. When you feel you have identified the actions needed to move your project forward, take at least four initial passes at them in order to create a coherent plan.

1. In the first pass, sort your actions (irrespective of the specific Renewal Coaching element from which they come) according to what should happen in the first twenty-five days, the second twenty-five days, the third twenty-five days, and then the last twenty-five days. When you do this, you are likely to play back and forth between the strengths and weaknesses revealed by your Renewal Coaching assessments.
2. In the second pass, order the actions within each of the four quarters.
3. Take a third pass at your work so far and reconcile any action that now appears to be out of place, missing, or redundant.
4. In your fourth pass, add dates to each action, beginning with today's date and working toward one hundred days from now.

Determine Your Timeline

Look at a calendar and note the first hundred days of your project. You can download a 100-Day Renewal Project template from www.RenewalCoaching.com, or you can make your own. Identify obvious dates for actions that involve progress monitoring of significant indicators. As you become clearer on the other actions you will take to move this project forward, you will continue to populate the timeline with dates and specific actions to elicit renewal.

____

____

____

____

____

____

____

____

People and Networks to Involve

The final element of your 100-Day Renewal Project is the identification of the people, networks, and alliances you will work with to accomplish the goals of your plan. As you do this, it is important to remember that the 100-Day Renewal Project is personal, and it is the main tool that clients and coaches use in each coaching conversation. As such, the actions that populate the plan should demand much from the client leader, and they should not simply be actions that are delegated wholesale to other people. They are actions that the leader should be intimately involved in within the first hundred days, and they should involve the work of other people and networks.

Identify People and Networks

Use the following space to brainstorm the individuals, teams, and networks essential to collaborate with as you move your project forward.

Individuals:

____

____

____

Teams:

____

____

____

Networks:

____

____

____

FINAL COMMENTS ABOUT YOUR 100-DAY RENEWAL PROJECT PLAN

Remember, 100-Day Renewal Project plans are living documents that capture your best thinking as you or the leaders you coach outline the high-powered actions that can guarantee success. Throughout the coaching engagement, the leader will revise actions in the plan as new information is available and in response to events that occur day to day.

CHAPTER 7

Coaching Essentials

Renewal Coaching provides a model for leadership coaching in which research and ideas about sustainable change are applied to the coaching context. It emphasizes in particular the contention that sustainable change for individuals and organizations always involves the process of renewal and is associated with the pursuit of a greater good. Successful practice of Renewal Coaching requires attention to seven elements: recognition, reality, reciprocity, resilience, resonance, relationships, and renewal.

Whether you are a coach who works inside an organization, a leader who uses coaching as an approach for developing the people with whom you work, or an independent professional coach, the techniques in this chapter will help you focus on how to integrate the Renewal Coaching perspectives into your current coaching work. You will reflect on your current approach to coaching and the tools you use to compare and improve your coaching practices aided by the perspectives of the Renewal Coaching framework.

THE BASIC COACHING FRAMEWORK

Coaching is a process for supporting individuals and organizations in making positive changes. The foundations of great coaching are clear, and although terminology may differ, coaches around the globe recognize the essential elements that compose the basic coaching framework:

- *Agreement:* How will the coach and client work together?
- *Assessment:* What are the client's strengths and challenges?
- *Focus:* What does the client want to accomplish?
- *Conversations:* What process guides the coaching conversation?
- *Project management:* How will clients accomplish their goals?
- *Accountability:* How will the coach and client each know they have done their part?
- *Reflection:* How will the coach and client think about what they have learned on this journey, and how will they take this wisdom into the future?

How Strong Is Your Framework?

Reflect on how you use or intend to use each of the basic coaching elements in your coaching. Use the following table:

	Process in place? Yes or No	**If yes, describe your process here**	**If no, I will take these steps to put this element in place**
Establish the Agreement			
Assessment			
Coaching Focus			
The Coaching Conversation			
Project Management			
Accountability			
Reflection			

Skills Used by Coaches

Just as coaches recognize the need for an overarching framework to implement coaching practices successfully, they also embrace and mindfully apply very specific skills as they coach. This is true for coaches who are internal and those who are external to the organization, as well as for leaders who use coaching as a process to develop the people they work with. The essential skills used by every coach are:

- Listening
- Asking mediating questions
- Voicing theories
- Testing hypotheses
- Giving and receiving feedback
- Brainstorming and calling for action

Of all of these, listening is the primary skill used by coaches. Because coaches are often people who have also served as consultants, speakers, advisors, and leaders, they are frequently very articulate and possess enormous expertise and are understandably eager to share their ideas with clients. Nevertheless, the coach is most effective when listening. Indeed, this is a critical distinction between consultants and coaches, with the former ending sentences with periods (and a bit too frequently with exclamation points) and the latter ending sentences with question marks. Without diligent focus on the skill of asking questions that generate meaningful reflection, the practical value of everything else the coach has to offer will evaporate. Without successful listening, the coach can offer brilliant insights to the wrong person on the wrong subject. Without effective listening, coaches can damage a relationship rather than support it. People who are new to coaching sometimes find this emphasis on listening surprising because they mistakenly believe that coaches must be smooth talkers who know exactly what to do and exactly how to say it to persuade clients to do the one magic thing that will work. The problem is, coaches are not in the business of telling clients what to do—that's called consulting. Coaches listen, really listen. That means they resist nothing, judge nothing, add nothing, change nothing from what the client says. If change is to occur, the client makes the change; the coach does not direct the change. Coaches listen to understand the client so that, as the coaching conversation moves forward, they interact within the client's world. If they fail to do this, the coaches are, by default, giving advice or speaking from their own experience.

Best Case: Listening

Think of an interaction with a client, coworker, or family member in which the way you listened to them made a difference. Describe first what you did and then the quality of the effect on the other person.

What I did:

____

____

____

The impact this had:

____

____

____

Mediating questions are often provocative in that they stir emotion and stimulate activity. Renewal Coaches ask mediating questions to provoke actions toward the seven elements: recognition, reality, reciprocity, resilience, resonance, relationship, and renewal.

Best Case: Mediating Questions

Think of an interaction with a client, coworker, or family member in which the way you used mediating questions made a difference for them. Describe first what you did and then the quality of the effect on the other person.

What I did:

____

____

____

The impact this had:

____

____

____

Especially during the brainstorming stage of the coaching conversation, coaches contribute ideas and share their reactions. Often they phrase these ideas as questions or theories. For example, they might say something like this: "People tend to react this way when they believe they don't have control over the situation. Do you think that is happening here?"

A theory is a statement that consistently explains the relationship between causes and effects. Sometimes a theory has been supported by exceptional amounts of evidence over time and therefore is accepted as a consistent explanation of events. The "theory of gravity" falls into this category. Other times, however, the term *theory* is associated with contemplation and informed speculation. Unlike gravity (every time you jump out a window you are going to descend to the pavement, not ascend to the clouds), theories about human relationships are associated with observations and evidence that may be very consistent, but they are not in the same category of scientific certainty. That is why words such as *always* and *never* are unhelpful in coaching conversations. However, if we are willing to accept a middle ground between idle speculation and mysticism, on the one hand, and scientific certainty, on the other, then theory generation plays an important role in coaching.

Best Case: Voicing Theories

Think of an interaction with a client, coworker, or family member in which the theories you offered made a difference for them. Describe first what you did and then the quality of the effect on the other person.

What I did:

____

____

____

The impact this had:

____

____

____

Coaches give feedback with the goal of empowering clients and helping them to reflect on their efficacy. Coaches never give feedback to get something off their chest or to manipulate the client to act in accordance with what the coach feels is the best course of action. Coaches always give feedback as a way to support clients and help them learn. Feedback is often a catalyst to clients discovering what their next step will be.

Best Case: Giving Feedback

Think of an interaction with a client, coworker, or family member in which the way you provided feedback made a difference for them. Describe first what you did and then the quality of the effect on the other person.

What I did:

____

____

____

____

The impact this had:

____

____

____

____

Exhibit 7.1 Basic Coaching Skills

	Rating 1–5	Questions I have about using these skills effectively with clients	Infused with Renewal Coaching Elements: Recognition, Reality, Reciprocity, Resilience, Resonance, Relationship, and Renewal
Listening			
Asking Mediating Questions			
Voicing Theories			
Giving Feedback			

Use Exhibit 7.1 to reflect on your current proficiency with the basic coaching skills and how it could change to reflect the seven elements of the Renewal Coaching framework.

- Step 1: Rate yourself on a scale of 1 to 5, with 1 representing low proficiency in the skill and 5 representing expert status with the skill.
- Step 2: Write out the questions that come to mind for this skill, related to your coaching proficiency. (For example, How do I know which mediating question to ask a client? How do I ask clarifying questions without derailing the flow of my client's thoughts? When does feedback do more harm than good? How do I voice theories without sounding like I am manipulating my client toward a course of action?)
- Step 3: Reflect on how the Renewal Coaching paradigm influences each skill.

VALUES OF THE RENEWAL COACH

Effective coaches are driven by values that maintain the integrity of coaching and offer some guarantee to clients that what good coaches say and do within the coaching relationship are influenced by values that promote positive outcomes. For example, effective coaches hold values of confidentiality, trust, empowerment, accountability, respect, and commitment to the client's goals.

Your Coaching Values

What values guide you in what you say and do as a coach? Write as many as you can think of in the space below:

____

____

____

____

____

Renewal Coaching Values

Each element of the Renewal Coaching framework (recognition, reality, reciprocity, resilience, resonance, relationship, and renewal) suggests an associated set of values that give strength and focus to coaching work. Table 7.1 provides a brief description of each of the values that must be embraced by a Renewal Coach and explains the relationship between each value and the elements of the Renewal Coaching model. Take some time to reflect on the values on the basis of your understanding of the Renewal Coaching perspective so far. As you progress through Chapters Eight through Fourteen and come to understand more about the Renewal Coaching perspective, please return to this page and add any new insights, questions, and ideas.

Acceptance

Renewal Coaches accept clients wherever they are in the process of renewal, without judgment and without consequence. This does not mean that the Renewal Coach does not engage many great coaching skills, including dialogue, probing, confronting, and accountability. Rather, no matter how

Table 7.1 Renewal Coaching Values

Renewal Coaching Element	Description	Corresponding Renewal Coaching Values
R1 Recognition	Identify *what* must change	Acceptance Humility
R2 Reality	*Acknowledge* how ideal and real states differ	Openness
R3 Reciprocity	*Share* mutual experiences and vulnerabilities	Honesty Respect Service
R4 Resilience	*Bounce back* from pain	Suffering with meaning Equifinality
R5 Relationship	The *personal* elements of coaching	Every conversation matters Accountability
R6 Resonance	Leadership and *emotional intelligence*	Compassion Mindfulness
R7 Renewal	Finding *energy* to complete the journey	The greater good Redemption

clients respond, the Renewal Coach meets them wherever they are with compassion.

Acceptance is also a mind-set that Renewal Coaches teach their clients as they address important issues in the client's life and work. It is all about seeing data clearly without labeling the data as good or bad and instead considering it information. In this context, acceptance implies a candid and realistic orientation to the world. The value of acceptance helps coaches and clients to consider their emotional reactions while avoiding the negative impact that emotionalism can have on vision and judgment. This value allows the coaches and clients to see clearly what needs to change.

Humility

Humility allows Renewal Coaches to question certainty. This value implies that one does not know everything in every situation—hardly a stunning statement, but one too rarely acknowledged in many organizations. Humility guides people to slow down and ask if there is anything else they need to know. They are not asking, "What's wrong with this picture?" but rather "What's missing in this picture?"

Renewal Coaches apply the value of humility throughout the coaching relationship. It is a value that reminds them that listening is the most important coaching skill. Humility allows Renewal Coaches to maintain presence and stay in the moment with their clients. Their minds are not racing ahead and seeking the answers, for they know that the answers will come through the relationship, not through shallow displays of the knowledge of the coach.

Clients learn the value of humility in their own work through the relationship they have with their coach. They increase the amount of time they spend listening to other people. They stop themselves from saying things merely to demonstrate that they are correct, and pause to wonder what other data might be needed in order to make a better decision. Humility is crucial for recognizing what could change for the better in the organization.

Openness

Openness works hand in glove with humility. Renewal Coaches demonstrate openness with clients by asking questions that stimulate ideas, dreams, and outcomes that make a difference. It frees coaches to relinquish their past work and life experiences and to help clients visualize results that are remarkable for them in their organization. Openness implies that both coach and client are not defensive about what must change in order to realize those possibilities.

Clients demonstrate openness as they navigate the process of change leading to renewal. Throughout the Renewal Coaching experience, clients flexibly embrace unique approaches to problem solving, letting go of limiting beliefs and generating novel ideas.

Honesty

Renewal Coaches and clients demonstrate the value of honesty at many levels. Like any great relationship, the coaching relationship depends on both parties being honest with each other about what is working and not working, as well as being honest with themselves about how they contribute to the relationship. One of the most difficult skills for coaches is the ability to speak hard truths to clients. It takes courage and finesse to tell someone that they dropped the ball on an important task, neglected to prepare for an important conversation, or have the habit of putting down coworkers. Coaches must also provide honest and specific feedback to clients when things are going well. This is a way to build resilience and efficacy in the client. Coaches also must ask for and be open to honest feedback from the client. Asking the client how beneficial the coaching sessions are is one way to do this on a regular basis.

As they learn to trust their coaches, Renewal Coaching clients become comfortable in facing their own hard truths. They recognize when they need to face something difficult and they speak more easily about what is difficult for them.

Respect

Robb and Kathy Bocchino of Heart of Change, Inc., break down the word *respect* in this way: *spect* (to see), *re* (again). In essence they say that to respect another person is to see them again *as if it were the first time, each time.* This definition fits particularly well in the Renewal Coaching model. It invites both coach and client to treat each conversation as a fresh opportunity to listen with an open mind. It conveys a deep sense of faith in the abilities of both parties in the coaching relationship to understand their role and summon the knowledge, skills, and dispositions required in the moment. Listening is an obvious and visible manifestation of respect. Following through on commitments is another.

As clients experience respect in the reciprocal nature of the Renewal Coaching process, so too do they bring respect to other relationships at work and in life. They listen better and give up grudges more easily. They assume positive intent and give people the benefit of the doubt, at least until they prove otherwise.

Service

Sometimes a Renewal Coach has deep experience and expertise in the field of their clients. This poses a challenge for many coaches because the temptation to coach from one's own past is particularly strong. Although clients appear relieved at times when coaches hang out the consulting shingle and give advice, this relief is usually short-lived. Advice too frequently comes from the past. It is good only to the extent that the current situation mirrors the situation from the past. In complex organizations, the differences between people, cultures, and processes result in nuances in the reality of the situation. Coaches who hold the value of service make it a point to understand clients and their organizations. This occurs only through listening and setting aside assumptions. A service orientation allows Renewal Coaches to challenge clients to identify goals in service of a greater good for their organizations and the people in them.

A sense of service usually elevates the goals of clients from something on a to-do list to something that leads to a remarkable outcome for the organization. Results for a greater good might be a new process, or an entirely new structure.

Suffering with Meaning

When it rains it pours. There is no escape from the adversities of life. Some people, however, face the difficulties of life with wisdom instead of surrender. They face these challenges directly, resisting nothing, feeling free to experiment with new responses, awakening to new insights, considering the needs of others, and taking action that turns the entire mess into something better than existed before. All of us have wisdom even if we do not use it in every situation. As they relate to their clients, Renewal Coaches model this value through words and actions. Meaning diminishes suffering and allows a person to bounce back and find a new way of moving forward.

Clients in a Renewal Coaching relationship have chosen to create a result for the greater good. On their journey toward the greater good, clients are likely to face antagonistic forces, perplexing choices, and paralyzing self-doubt. Renewal Coaches have the important role of guiding clients to find meaning in each setback and disappointment. In time, clients begin to seek and find meaning themselves. As they process each important event with their coach, clients arrive at new and helpful insights that give them energy and courage to take the next step.

Equifinality

Equifinality is a principle from open systems theory that indicates the existence of many different pathways to the same outcome (Cummings & Worley, 2005; Weisbord, 1987). Renewal Coaches follow the pathway taken by their clients. They respect the self-determination of their clients and the meaning that clients make of the challenges of their lives.

Clients take away from the coaching experience and into the organization a healthy respect for equifinality. Because of their own experience, they awaken to the variety of pathways to excellence taken by others in the organization. This perspective invites openness to ideas, creativity, and endless pathways to resilience. This value often leads directly to the legacy created by the leader.

Every Conversation Matters

Every relationship is a series of conversations. Imagine the implications if we all treated conversations as if they mattered. Renewal Coaches build relationships by treating every conversation as important. From being on time for the meeting, to following through on promises, to remembering what matters most to the client, the Renewal Coach builds and sustains a safe and respectful relationship in which clients can do the work they want to do.

A remarkable thing happens when people are experiencing Renewal Coaching. People around them begin to notice that they are different. They listen more and talk less. They notice the emotions of other people and attend to the subtext and nonverbal cues in conversations. They ask the right questions at precisely the right times, and they do not jump in to solve problems unless invited to do so. The relationship of Renewal Coaching goes beyond the coach and client and includes the organization itself.

Accountability

Renewal Coaching provides equal amounts of support and accountability. Because coaching is a development tool to support people as they take action for meaningful change, it is both gentle and tough. Renewal Coaches will always accept their clients, but they will never let them be complacent, make excuses, or give up. They would rather sever the relationship and agree that Renewal Coaching is not right at this time than allow a client who chooses a victim orientation to remain that way.

At the same time, clients expect coaches to do their part. They want coaches to treat them with respect and accountability, and they expect coaches to follow through on commitments and promises. In time, clients begin to see how helpful and effective this balance is if they apply it with the people with whom they work. They begin to inspire others toward the greater good as well.

Compassion

Boyatzis and McKee (2005) explain that compassion is a manifestation of being in tune with the needs and wants of other people and then being "motivated to act on our feelings" (p. 77). Compassion sustains Renewal Coaches in their practice. Without compassion for the needs of others who want to make a difference in the world, the Renewal Coach would soon find other work.

In turn, compassion is a driving force motivating the client in creating a greater good. During the Renewal Coaching process, coaches support their clients in delving into questions that reveal the needs and wants of others. Although the nature of wisdom is frequently debated, almost everyone agrees that wisdom creates a common good—a result that supports the needs of the greatest number of people over a sustained period.

Mindfulness

Achieving a greater good cannot be left to chance. It represents such significant and notable change either in process or in result that a trail of specific, strategic, and mindful actions can be documented and marveled at by all. In the Zen tradition, mindfulness is sometimes described as feeling the floor under your feet (Shoshanna, 2003). During times of stress, when we are more likely to respond simply on the basis of old habits and patterns, mindfulness is especially important. It causes us to slow down, feel the ground underneath our feet, and consider where we are and who we are relative to all the chaos spinning around us. Mindfulness is the antidote to reaction. This value requires Renewal Coaches to remain mindful in their own lives as well as in their coaching relationships. It asks coaches to consider their own emotions, intuition, physical sensations, and wisdom. A Renewal Coach does this before each coaching call or meeting with a client by taking some time to settle or temporarily quiet troubling issues in their own lives, even as they ready themselves to be fully present for the client.

Clients surface the value of mindfulness for themselves as they work with their coach to challenge assumptions, think things through, gather additional information, and tune in to their own emotions, intuition, and physical sensations.

The Greater Good

Today, in business and in life, people can find a coach to help them achieve a variety of personal and professional objectives. Some people want to lose weight, some want to be better organized, some want to be a better boss or a better partner in a romantic relationship. Renewal Coaching operates from the central premise of a belief in the greater good. Renewal Coaches support their clients in achieving something remarkable that influences others as well. Sometimes this is simply a matter of perspective. The person who wants to lose weight can do so through a fairly simple formula—eat less, move more—but they can also extend the outcome to include living a long and productive life in order to be a better parent or grandparent who can influence future generations.

Clients in a Renewal Coaching relationship learn to take disappointments in stride. They no longer see every small issue as equally important to the big issues. They are able to differentiate between that which needs to be accomplished and that which positively changes a difficult situation.

Redemption

The value of redemption is clear in the Renewal Coaching process when the greater good becomes more important than the exigencies of the moment. This does not mean merely having a positive attitude in the face of adversity. Stoicism is a trait revered in popular culture, but it is essentially counterfeit, covering an unpopular visage with one that is socially acceptable. Redemption is a change not in appearance but in belief, the transformation of adversity into blessing. The next exercise asks you to connect personally with the values that undergird the Renewal Coaching approach. Putting yourself in the position of Renewal Coach, record your insights about how these values would influence what you say and do while coaching.

Reflection on Renewal Coaching Values

1. Recognition: identifying *what* must change

   Corresponding values: acceptance and humility

My reflections on how these values influence Renewal Coaches as they focus their client on recognition:

____

____

____

____

2. Reality: acknowledging how ideal and real states differ

   Corresponding value: openness

My reflections on how this value influences Renewal Coaches as they focus their client on reality:

____

____

____

3. Reciprocity: sharing mutual experiences and vulnerabilities

   Corresponding values: honesty, respect, service

My reflections on how these values influence Renewal Coaches as they focus their client on reciprocity:

____

____

____

____

____

____

(continued)

Reflection on Renewal Coaching Values (continued)

4. Resilience: bouncing back from pain

   Corresponding values: suffering with meaning, acceptance

My reflections on how these values influence Renewal Coaches as they focus their client on resilience:

____

____

____

____

5. Resonance: finding the energy to complete the journey

   Corresponding values: compassion, mindfulness

My reflections on how these values influence Renewal Coaches as they focus their client on resonance:

____

____

____

____

6. Relationship: focusing on the personal elements of coaching

   Corresponding values: every conversation matters, accountability

My reflections on how these values influence Renewal Coaches as they focus their client on relationship:

____

____

____

____

Reflection on Renewal Coaching Values (continued)

7. Renewal: finding energy to complete the journey

   Corresponding values: the greater good, redemption

My reflections on how these values influence Renewal Coaches as they focus their client on renewal:

____

____

____

____

CONCLUSION

Renewal Coaching gives coaches and leaders who use coaching in their work a paradigm for using the coaching process to cause sustainable change. As coaches who embrace the Renewal Coaching perspective continue to use the fundamental coaching processes and tools, the content and quality of the coaching conversation engages the seven elements of the Renewal Coaching framework. For example, client projects will have a greater good as their focus, mediating questions will address the seven Renewal Coaching elements, and the actions that clients design will activate learning, evidence, attitudes, and decisions that are clearly guided by the principles of Renewal Coaching.

Our most sincere hope is that whether you are new to coaching or a veteran coach seeking to grow and revitalize your coaching practice, you will discover the leverage of using the Renewal Coaching perspective to coach in a way that leads to sustainable change for individuals and organizations.

PART THREE

Reflection

CHAPTER 8

Recognition
Finding Patterns of Toxicity and Renewal

The essence of recognition is the identification of patterns. Renewal Coaching is helpful because individuals tend to focus on and react to events in the present, whereas an effective coach can help them identify similarities among seemingly isolated incidents. Some patterns can be positive, such as listening, fact gathering, and a willingness to consider alternatives before coming to a conclusion. Other patterns can be toxic, such as the presumption of bad faith, coming to conclusions without evidence, or at the other extreme, the unfiltered acceptance of the claims of others without critical thinking. To break out of a destructive pattern, clients must master the skills of pattern recognition and formative inquiry. In this chapter you will apply these skills to challenges in your personal and professional environment. First you will review the results of your own assessment. Then we will consider the cases of two clients facing different challenges in the recognition element of the Renewal Coaching framework. Next you will be guided through two interactive exercises—one if recognition is a strength for you, another if recognition is not a strength. Finally you will identify specific action steps to integrate into your 100-Day Renewal Project.

Recognition Assessment Review

Take a moment to review your Recognition Assessment from Chapter Four. If you have not yet taken the assessment, please do so by logging on to www.RenewalCoaching.com and selecting Assessments.

My Recognition Assessment score: ____________________

Key insights from my responses to open-ended questions in the Recognition Assessment:

____

____

____

RENEWAL MOMENTS

Reuben was a master of destructive emotions (Goleman, 2003), making an instant leap from observation to judgment, fear, anger, jealousy, and rage. An inadvertent slight from a colleague became, through the lens of Reuben's emotional judgment, an intentional insult. Cancellation of a meeting for the most benign of reasons was transformed by Reuben into the inevitable conclusion that he was worthless and unable to make a meaningful contribution at work.

Allie's nonprofit organization represented the opposite of Reuben's angry antagonism. Allie, her board, and a cadre of enthusiastic volunteers were full of optimism and good intentions. They saw the silver lining in every cloud, took on every challenge, accepted every invitation to service, and never failed to take on more than was humanly or organizationally possible. Their board agendas were crowded to the point that they never finished meetings on time or completed an agenda. The minutes of the past year's meetings revealed a litany of good intentions and enthusiastic project initiatives, but there was not a single bit of evidence that a major project had been completed. Allie reveled in her role of "brainstormer in chief" and enjoyed discussions over a few glasses of wine about how she would change the world. However, her proliferating good intentions prevented Allie and her organization from gaining focus or implementing action. As a result, apparently cheerful Allie was subject to bouts of despair.

Additionally her board's optimism was deteriorating by the day and didn't know where Allie's next paycheck would come from. Without a history of accomplishment, their grant funding was in jeopardy. They had so many good ideas that they didn't know where to start, and therefore became immobilized. Allie's life felt chaotic and out of control as she confronted the disparity between her good intentions and the reality of her inactivity.

Does either of these patterns ring a bell? Can you think of times when you have been excessively pessimistic and judgmental, jumping to conclusions too quickly? Or perhaps you can recall times when you have been duped, taken advantage of by a person who preyed on your goodwill and optimistic outlook. In isolation, these errors in judgment are part of our humanity. When repeated and taken to extremes, however, these errors present an opportunity to improve our skills of pattern recognition.

With the support of their Renewal Coaches, Reuben and Allie are leading strikingly different lives today because they have mastered the art of recognizing destructive patterns. In the past, Reuben focused on catastrophic thoughts of the future whereas Allie entertained unrealistic fantasies. Neither of them could make the leap from a rational assessment of today's actions to a meaningful future. Today, by contrast, Reuben and Allie consciously engage in formative thought processes by challenging themselves to stop, identify patterns, and examine the link between today and a realistic future. Reuben could not focus on the greater good because he was obsessed with personal insults; Allie could not achieve the greater good because she and her organization were overwhelmed and paralyzed. Having learned the value of pattern recognition and formative inquiry, they stop and ask questions, sometimes exploring their responses with their coach and other times writing their analyses in their journals. These conversations and journal entries serve to interrupt destructive patterns and reorient Allie and Reuben toward the path of renewal.

RECOGNITION IN ACTION

Take a few moments to explore patterns that you observe in your own life. Complete the following worksheet by responding in writing to the questions proposed in each phase of the STOP technique.

The STOP Technique

S: Situation

Think of a situation in your life that you associate with destructive emotions. What happened? Who were the people involved? Did it happen at work, at home, or in volunteer activities? Provide as many details as you can.

T: Test Assumptions

What assumptions did you make about the people involved, their motives, and other reasons for their behavior?

O: Opposing Interpretations

What is at least one alternative interpretation of the same situation? What other explanations of behavior might be valid? What other motives might the people in this situation have had?

P: Pattern Recognition

What do you notice about the pattern of your reaction to the situation? Are your assumptions about the causes of the behavior of other people similar to what you have experienced in the past?

IF RECOGNITION IS A STRENGTH

Many readers are surprised that a high score on the recognition assessment is not necessarily a strength. Too high a score suggests excessive skepticism and overgeneralization, and too low a score suggests a potential for indecisiveness. If you scored in the middle range, you have a thoughtful blend of skepticism and reason. To capitalize on this strength, you can wear your mistakes proudly on your sleeve. You might even make a list of "my top ten bone-headed mistakes" to show your colleagues and subordinates, with a smile, that you have learned from past errors. Perhaps in the past you were overly critical and magnified a single mistake of a colleague into a huge and unchangeable character flaw. Perhaps you didn't question enough and allowed yourself to be misled because of insufficient data. By confidently sharing your own mistakes and your growth in pattern recognition, you can help clients and colleagues understand that your strength in recognition is not a mark of cognitive superiority but simply the result of your diligent development of a skill.

Here's the most challenging part about having recognition for a strength: other people might think, "She's just amazing—it's just a gift from the gods." You know better. In fact, your skills in pattern recognition allow you to draw inferences from your history of successes and failures, and although you don't enjoy failure any more than the next person, you have created a habit of transforming almost every failure into a learning experience. To further capitalize on this strength, complete Exhibit 8.1 and identify what you learned and what patterns you have observed.

Exhibit 8.1 My Three Biggest Mistakes

Biggest Mistakes	Lessons Learned	Patterns Observed

Rolland wears his brilliance on his sleeve. Finishing his doctoral dissertation before his twenty-fifth birthday, he published more than many of his more experienced colleagues before he was thirty. On paper, at least, Rolland is an expert in pattern recognition. His statistical training allows him to draw order from chaos in complex data sets. In the past few years, Rolland has also been able to apply his prodigious gifts to interpersonal relationships at work and at home. It was not always so. In his twenties, Rolland could not hide his brilliance, even when it was irrelevant to the social context. He alienated friends, colleagues, and lovers with his unceasing attempts to impress them with his intellectual prowess, when they simply wanted to engage him as a human. A reluctant client, Rolland was not enthusiastic about making a list of his greatest mistakes. But with a good deal of encouragement, he started to list them—almost all of them involved broken relationships. "I was pretty sure that the first three were the fault of other people," Rolland concluded. "But by the time the list exceeded twelve, even I had to admit that there was something more than the bad judgment of other people at work here." Slowly Rolland listed his lessons learned: "People don't like it when I point out their mistakes, even if I was just trying to help. Women are not impressed with my petty victories at work. I need the cooperation, love, and respect of others, and I can't achieve those things through intimidation and imperious demands." When Rolland confronted the right column in Exhibit 8.1, a pattern slowly emerged. As a statistician, Rolland had been trained to look for patterns and they came easily to him. In this case, the tough part of the problem was identifying what was not there. Among all of the friends, colleagues, family members, lovers, and enemies he had listed, and amid all of the lessons he thought he had learned, there was not a hint, not a syllable, that suggested a consideration of the feelings of others. The only lens through which he had viewed these lessons previously was, "What's in it for me?" He saw for the first time that this singular focus was part of the problem.

IF RECOGNITION IS A WEAKNESS

There is a clinical term for people like you who sometimes overgeneralize and other times fail to come to a conclusion as they await better evidence: "normal." So stop beating yourself up and acknowledge that skill in recognition is not mystical insight but a skill that you can acquire, as surely as you have acquired other skills that give you confidence and comfort. To improve your skills in recognition, start with some introspection about your strengths.

Consider the case of Tamika. Too frequently people believe that their successes and achievements have been the result of character traits, the kindness of others, or mystical influences. If these assumptions were true, then your successes could not be replicated. To complete Exhibit 8.2, consider the successes that have been repeated throughout your life. Think in particular of something you did well as a child, something you did well in early adulthood, and something that you do well now. What specifically are the patterns of behavior and belief that have led to these successes?

For example, one client, Tamika, loved to put on musical and dance variety shows as a kid. She would create the theme of the show, write the skits, recruit the participants, teach them their parts, send invitations, sell the brownies and popcorn, secure the space for guests and the stage, print the programs, host the event, and perform the show—all in the time of a summer afternoon. A decade later, Tamika was still a multitasker, finishing her degree

Exhibit 8.2 Learning from Success

Consistent Success	Behavior Associated with Success	Beliefs Associated with Success

while working two jobs and volunteering in her church. Now in her forties, she publishes articles, books, and newsletters; coaches leaders in many disciplines; travels internationally; and finds time for friends, family, and animals. She carries out these tasks fueled by a belief that her work has value, whether or not those around her share that belief. Just as some of her comedy routines fell flat when she was eleven, some of the ideas she presented to professors at age twenty-one were received without enthusiasm. She has written articles that received rave reviews, but she has worked equally hard on articles that did not elicit a single comment. In Exhibit 8.2 Tamika might list as a consistent success her willingness to take risks and organize large and complex projects. The behaviors associated with these successes include a high level of vision, planning, energy, and organization. Her belief system is characterized by an indomitable confidence that whatever embarrassment may be associated with a failure today will be more than offset by tomorrow's success. Her infectious enthusiasm has become a self-fulfilling prophesy as both Tamika and her colleagues have learned to expect that she will be successful.

If Tamika had believed that she simply was "talented," then her first experience with disappointment, disapproval, and criticism might have suggested to her that her talent had evaporated. Because Tamika's belief was not in talent but in hard work, enthusiasm, planning, and execution, she created lifelong patterns of behaviors and beliefs that have served her well. As Tamika contemplates the next phase of her life, she is sustained by the fact that her early successes were the result not of luck but rather of her ability to recognize the pattern of success that developed from her actions and beliefs.

NEXT STEPS IN THE 100-DAY RENEWAL PROJECT

In Chapter Six you started your 100-Day Renewal Project. You already have in mind the context of the greater good, the results that will transcend your immediate personal and organizational objectives. Now it is time to identify specific action steps inspired by your reflections on this chapter. Table 8.1

Table 8.1 Sample Action Steps in a 100-Day Renewal Project

Action Steps	People and Networks Engaged
Gather information on three recent team successes: What were the challenges? What were the results? Who was involved? What unexpected obstacles were encountered? Note that this is only information gathering, not analysis, evaluation, or judgment.	Technology team Marketing team Client service team
Identify lessons learned: List common elements of the team's successes.	Cross-functional analytical team
Identify patterns of resources: Examine the money, time, people, technology, and other resources for each project success.	Accounting, time sheets, human resources
Identify patterns of attitudes: Examine the emotional context of the team members and leaders for each project.	Confidential focus group of team members
Review twenty action items from the board of directors, meetings of the previous twelve months. For each action item, identify the follow-through: action successfully completed, action in progress, action deliberately deferred, or action neglected.	Board minutes, executive action plans, quarterly performance objective reports
Identify six successful and six unsuccessful one-to-one meetings.	Calendar, subordinates, colleagues
Identify patterns of success: time of day, duration of meetings, agenda, focus, relevance to vision and mission.	Coach and personal reflection

provides some sample steps in a 100-Day Renewal Project that bear directly on recognition.

Write down your own action steps in the following table using the LEAD technique introduced in Chapter Six:

What do you need to LEARN?

What EVIDENCE do you need to collect and analyze?

What ATTITUDES and expectations must be developed?

What DECISIONS must be made?

Action Steps	People and Networks Engaged

COACHING CONVERSATION

"This was brutal," Allie said to her coach after the latest board meeting. "Why do you think so?" her coach replied. "I thought you just told me that you were getting to some very important insights."

"That's true," Allie continued. "I shared with the board the work I've been doing about recognizing patterns, both in my own work and in their work. I provided a list—four pages of it—of our collective brainstorms of the past year, all taken directly from our minutes."

"That must have been interesting," said her coach.

"Interesting is not exactly the word I would have used—more like terrifying and embarrassing. It's clear that all of us are better at starting things than at finishing them. Of the more than sixty new ideas we've developed in the past year, the objective truth is that we have completed only three of them. But because the board and I have been so fragmented in our attention, so full of enthusiasm about new ideas, we didn't realize that our actual accomplishments had been pretty minimal. I feel awful."

"Tell me a little more about the three projects that you did complete," said the coach.

"Actually, they were pretty wonderful—a new Mom's day out for low-income parents, a mentoring program for teen mothers, and the new young man's club for sixth-grade boys without fathers at home. Each of them really has a significant impact." Allie started to sound a bit more calm and hopeful.

"This sounds terrific," replied the coach. "What made those three projects successful? What was different about them?"

"It's hard to quantify," continued Allie. "If you could just see the faces on the people we serve, just a single one is enough to keep me going on my worst day. We're literally saving lives not just for our clients but for their kids and grandkids."

"I can tell that this means a lot to you. What specifically did you do that spelled the difference? Why were these projects successful and what was your role?"

"Okay, let me think. In fact, let me stop and look at my project notes. I guess the first thing that I'm noticing is that I actually have project notes for the successful projects. When I reviewed the board minutes, I found a lot of great ideas that were just that—great ideas without any follow-up. So the first thing the successful ideas had in common was that I put my ideas into writing about how to translate the concepts into action."

"Excellent," encouraged the coach. "What else do you notice?"

"Well, this is a bit troubling, but I can't avoid noticing that our operations director, Donald, isn't involved in a single one of these. He always seems busy—almost frantic—and some of our board members think he has a great work ethic, because of the long hours he puts in around the office. But the truth is he was not involved in any of these three successful projects. Frankly, I'm not sure what he's doing when he appears to be so busy, but it is clear to me now that he's not making the contribution to our success that he could."

"You're producing some good preliminary insights. What else do you notice?"

Allie thought for a moment. "Maybe this is the most important thing of all, which I should have noticed from the beginning. All of these projects are directly related to our mission of empowering, educating, and enriching the lives of others. These projects provided direct services to clients and nurtured one-to-one human relationships. The other projects—the ideas that sounded interesting but never led to meaningful action—were about organizational issues and grand strategies. The new database, computer network, strategic plan, and 'board of boards' that we thought would improve communication with other agencies have all been huge drains on time. Donald hogs the time at board meetings with endless progress reports on his unfinished projects, meets with consultants and vendors over long lunches, and he's always hurrying out the door to the board meetings of other organizations. But in the last year none of his projects have been finished, even though he conveys the impression at board meetings that action is imminent. It's starting to become clear to me now," Allie concluded. "We could plan every board meeting around two essential questions. First, do the items on the agenda support our mission? Second, are the items on the agenda ready for board action? Those two questions would eliminate a good deal of the progress reports from Donald, and general discussions from board members. I don't know if this will get us totally focused, but I know that next month we are going to have fewer items on the agenda, and that operating reports not ready for board discussion are going to come to me."

"That sounds like a plan," said the coach. "Just one last question. What's the worst that could happen if you take these actions?"

Let's pause for a moment. Before you read any further, consider your own reaction to what Allie has said. What other questions could you ask?

Are there other patterns that Allie might recognize? If so, what questions would you raise to help her consider those patterns?

Allie appears to have come to a significant conclusion. What could go wrong? How can you help her minimize the impact of a decision that is either abrupt or based on inadequate information?

"Well," Allie said slowly, "Donald is going to have hurt feelings. He's got personal relationships with a couple of board members and he may go to them directly to complain. But after reviewing the previous year's minutes during our last meeting, the vast majority of the board is as frustrated as I am and they expect me to take bold and decisive action. I'll do my best to explain my rationale to Donald and to the executive committee before the agenda is published, and I'll include a cover letter signed by the chairperson to explain the shift in agenda policy. We can also offer a 'post-meeting' operations briefing for those people who really want to stay around and hear more. But the real meetings are going to focus on our mission."

Allie's coaching conversation is just one step on a continuing journey toward renewal. Her consideration of detailed information, drawing of careful inferences, and willingness to take decisive action are evidence that Allie and her coach are using the recognition part of the Renewal Coaching framework well. Unfortunately, the real world is about to intrude into Allie's plans. Although she sees the matter clearly, her colleagues in the office and her board members have a long history of commitment to the way things have been. Even though the board is unhappy with the lack of focus and follow-through, and even though any objective consideration of the evidence would suggest that the changes Allie proposes are essential, the emotional barriers to change remain high. Allie will need to take on the role of coach with her board and employees to help them see the same patterns she has noticed. It will not be sufficient for her to lecture them about her insights. Rather, she must help to build their capacity for pattern recognition. She might begin by asking her staff to help her notice the patterns in Allie's own leadership behavior that are helpful and unhelpful, thus creating an opportunity to model a nondefensive reaction to pattern recognition. Then she can share the evidence she has examined and how everyone in the organization, including Allie, Donald, and every board member, can learn from their successes.

In the next chapter we examine the next part of the Renewal Coaching framework: reality. We meet another coach and client who are seeking hope, optimism, and compassion while at the same time keeping their minds focused on objective data. They are pulled in two different directions, with their hearts inclined toward optimism and their minds focused on what appears to be a more pessimistic reality. We will see that neither extreme is helpful, and we'll follow a coaching conversation that suggests that the heart/mind dichotomy is not any more helpful than other popular but unproductive divisions—Mars/Venus, left brain/right brain, manager/leader. Renewal Coaching helps clients to resist this sort of simplistic analysis of complex problems and instead see subtlety and nuance.

CHAPTER 9

Reality
Confronting Change Killers

If listening is the primary task of a coach, then the best way to engage in effective listening is for the coach to ask questions. When coaches help clients achieve reality, they create conversations that ask the client to compare the world as they see it to the evidence at hand. Facing reality may seem second nature to the seasoned executive who has devoted decades to examining evidence and comparing it to prevailing assertions. If these skills were so easily transferable, however, then attorneys, therapists, and accountants, all experts in their professional lives, would never face contradictions between their illusions and their behaviors. But lawyers who know the details of the laws against harassment can be jerks to a paralegal, therapists who write books about relationships can fail to maintain a successful marriage, and accountants who master the details of complex corporate obligations can fail to file their own income tax returns. We are hardly exempt from this phenomenon. As teachers who love children, we have lost patience with unruly kids; as leaders of organizations, we have criticized when we could have encouraged and provided direction. A focus on reality does not make one immune from these errors, but it does lead us to admit them. One of the leading thinkers, writers, and speakers on leadership for the past three decades, Tom Peters, hosted a week-long "skunk camp" for thirty-three organizational leaders from around the world. On the final evening, Tom gave his latest book to each of the participants and offered a few words of challenge. He said to Doug, "I don't think you're smarter than everybody else, but I do think you can make mistakes a lot faster." Although Peters is no diplomat, he is insightful, and his challenge to Doug gets at the heart of reality—make mistakes, admit them, learn from them—which is going to help you more than the pretense of intelligence.

Reality Assessment Review

Take a moment to review your Reality Assessment from Chapter Four. If you have not yet taken the assessment, please do so by logging on to www.RenewalCoaching.com and selecting Assessments.

My Reality Assessment score: ____________________

Key insights from my responses to the open-ended questions in the Reality Assessment:

____

____

____

____

____

REALITY MOMENTS

Dwight has been identified as a high-potential executive since he was a college intern at the firm where he now works. At twenty-nine, he was recently named the youngest vice president in the firm. His work ethic is legendary, and everyone knows he can be counted on to get things done, no matter how tight the deadline or how tough the challenge. Dwight's competence comes with a price, at least for those around him. He has always been a loner, and even as he assumes more responsibility in the organization, he is unwilling to share responsibilities with others. He has not kept an administrative assistant for more than eight months, declaring them all to be incompetent, a label he applies liberally to nearly everyone except himself and those above him in the organization. Dwight is incredibly competent—he types faster than any administrative assistant in the company (he insisted on taking their test to prove it), he knows technology better than many of the software technicians and contractors, and he can talk about the latest literature on leadership, management, manufacturing, and finance with anyone in the firm, or at least those with whom he is willing to have a conversation. Team meetings are typically a list of instructions and deadlines, followed by an abrupt demand for "Any questions?" in a manner that signals that he does not want to hear a single inquiry.

When Dwight was offered a coach, he was initially skeptical about the idea. "I got to where I am today without a coach," he said to the vice president in the human resources department. "Why do I need one now?" Reluctantly he agreed to have a conversation with a coach and, more reluctantly, agreed to have the coach speak confidentially with several of Dwight's subordinates and coworkers. Their first coaching conversation was not an easy one. When asked about the most satisfying part of his job, Dwight talked about teaching a management class at the university he had attended. "They ate it up with a spoon," said Dwight with evident pride. He had spoken eloquently to the class about his personal and corporate values, including respect for others. Best of all, a couple of the top students had spoken with him after the class to seek internships, and the professor had asked if he could send some of his graduates to Dwight for employment. These young people wanted, Dwight said, to be on his winning team. They even seemed to want to be like him, to learn the secrets of his young success.

"It sounds as if you enjoyed that quite a lot," the coach replied. "How have your experiences been with college interns in the past?"

"Awful," said Dwight, his tone changing from enthusiasm to contempt. "They're lazy, can't dress properly, and won't follow directions. They almost never last the summer."

"And what about your experiences with new employees?"

"Same thing—people just don't get it. I work hard and I expect others to do the same, but they don't. I have to check everything they say and review every detail."

Then the coach asked something that startled Dwight. "You seem pretty upset, even angry, about other people around you. How do you react when they disappoint you?"

Dwight confessed to being impatient, but he was not prepared when the coach asked about frequent incidents of Dwight's office behavior reported confidentially to the coach. As Dwight rose quickly through the ranks, yesterday's respected bosses became today's ordinary peers and tomorrow's disdained subordinates. His rages were legendary—he slammed doors, kicked trash baskets, threw paper, and cursed people until the air was blue.

"Who told you that?" demanded Dwight.

"We agreed that my conversations with your colleagues are confidential, just as my conversations with you are confidential," replied the coach. Thus began a series of coaching conversations in which Dwight began to consider not only his behavior but his beliefs about other people that led to his behavior. Certainly his primary belief was that he was a successful and high-achieving person, and therefore whatever he had done in the past, including being profoundly distrustful of other people, was part of that success. His reality assessment was nearly a "perfect" 100 points, and his written responses suggested that he was very close to burning out before his thirtieth birthday. In fact, although he loved talking about his success, he never felt successful. No job was prestigious enough, no office grand enough, no car elegant enough, and no girlfriend adoring enough. It wasn't Dwight's success that was at the core of his private belief, but his conviction that he was never successful enough.

Dwight represents one end of the reality continuum, characterized by cynicism, impatience, and anger. At the other end of the continuum is a gullibility that makes one vulnerable personally and professionally, exemplified by Boris. Everyone in the office uses "nice guy" to describe Boris, though it is not necessarily intended as a compliment. His department has endured some costly errors that, as the manager in charge of the project, he should have caught. He readily takes the blame for the mistakes of other people, and tolerates late arrivals and early departures, along with all manner of belligerent behavior, but nevertheless turns in routinely positive performance reviews. Boris is easily seduced by flattery at work and in his private life. He buys expensive gifts for girlfriends who care little for him and lavishes praise on employees who treat him with disrespect. Although most people would rather be around Boris than Dwight, neither of them offers a constructive approach to reality.

Are these caricatures exaggerated? Stanford professor Robert Sutton famously described the essence of building a civilized workplace in his book with a slightly scatological title (2007). The title (you can check the reference list if you're curious) was provoked by a faculty discussion of whether to hire a qualified but personally difficult researcher. "Listen," said one of Sutton's colleagues. "I don't care if that guy won the Nobel Prize. . . . I just don't want any assholes ruining our group" (p. 2). How many organizations claim the value of respect but tolerate inappropriate behavior on a regular basis? How many leaders talk a good game about civility and decency but publicly dress down an errant subordinate? The cost of our failure to face reality in the workplace is high, with consequences that are similar to harassment (Casciaro & Lobo, 2005) with regard to wasted time, emotional drain, and avoidance of personal and financial consequences.

Are there people in your life who are similar to Dwight and Boris? How do you feel about them?

____

____

____

____

____

IF REALITY IS A STRENGTH

A balanced score on the Reality Assessment is typically in the range of 41 to 70. This represents a nuanced view of reality in which you are neither cynical nor gullible. You blend appropriate skepticism with encouragement. Your skills can be particularly helpful in meetings where a group is considering alternatives to solve a problem. Your reality orientation allows you to encourage brainstorming without judgment and criticism, and at the same time to challenge people who make inappropriate or unsupported claims. Because these meetings may be dominated by others who are less self-effacing than you are, it is important that you stake your ground, even if by encouraging someone else rather than making your own point. If you have subordinates who justify bad behavior because they are being either "analytical" (meaning they are jerks) or "nice" (meaning they tolerate poor performance), then guide them to the balanced perspective you have. When their behavior is destructive, you will need to confront it. In dealing with bosses like Boris, you will need to take personal responsibility for your work, and not expect much in the way of constructive feedback. In dealing with a boss like Dwight, you will, like the rest of your colleagues, probably want to find a different place to work. You owe it to your employer to be candid in your exit interview about Dwight's destructive behavior.

Ways I can use strength in reality with colleagues:

____

____

____

IF REALITY IS A WEAKNESS

Although a coach may help to address differences between claims and evidence, the client may have deep-seated personality issues that would be more appropriately addressed in therapy than in coaching. A coach can help Dwight and Boris face reality by holding up a mirror so they can see more clearly their own actions and the effects they have on others. However, in these cases, there may be psychological issues that are beyond the purview of the coach. Even if the coach is trained as a psychologist, there are stark differences between coaching and psychotherapy, and engaging in the latter while claiming to perform the former violates the ethical boundaries of both professions. One recent estimate from the University of Sydney found that between 25 and 50 percent of those seeking coaching have "clinically significant levels of anxiety, stress or depression" (January 2009, p. 97; quoted in Coutu & Kauffman, 2009). If you suspect that this might apply to you, then consider an assessment for anxiety or depression either from a private provider or from the employee assistance program at your workplace. If you decide to see a therapist, be very clear about the goals and termination of the process. A good therapist will ask, "How will you know that we are finished?" You may want to consider a three-way conversation with your coach and therapist so that all parties are clear about the specific goals of coaching and you have a coherent and consistent approach to improving your performance.

If your score in the Reality Assessment was in the lower range, it suggests that you can take some immediate positive steps. First, practice appropriate challenges to inappropriate claims. This won't make you a cynic or a jerk. For example, if you have a colleague who routinely says, "Don't worry—it's all under control," and then frequently fails to deliver on her promises, you don't need to become angry or abusive, but you also do not need to acquiesce. You might, for example, say, "Actually, I am worried, so I'd like to ask you for a bit more clarity. Let's talk about exactly what you have completed on this project so far and let's review the actual work product; I really don't want to wait until the deadline next week to see it. Can we do that right now?" In the following table, list three examples of claims and questions. By writing down your response you will be better prepared. This is a new pattern of behavior, and it will take preparation and practice.

Inappropriate Claim	My Response

If your score on the Reality Assessment is in the higher range, you are probably thinking, "I'm not a jerk! I'm nothing like Dwight—and I'm certainly not the guy Professor Sutton was describing." True enough. The fact that you are taking time to engage in a systematic assessment suggests strongly that you are a reflective and thoughtful person. But it is probably reasonable to say that you are known for being a very smart, analytical, and challenging person. You might be proud of the fact that everyone knows that when they come into a meeting with you they had better be prepared, even overprepared, to answer what are sure to be rapid-fire and insightful questions from you. So, here is the question you must consider: Is it working? Do you find that as a result of your questioning nature and demanding style, your colleagues, subordinates, family members, and friends are wiser, more responsive, and better prepared this year than they were last year? Or do you think that things are actually getting worse? Are you in a cycle in which each time you ask tougher questions and then during the next encounter people are even less well prepared and you find yourself more and more frustrated? If this is the case, then consider the possibility that your very high reality score suggests that the costs of your analytical nature outweigh the benefits. In fact, because you are very intelligent and analytical, please complete the following exercise, listing in the left-hand column of the table the names of three people whose statements you find you regularly challenge. They might be outside professionals, subordinates, or even family members. In the middle column describe a recent encounter in which you challenged them. In the right-hand column describe how that challenge has or has not changed their behavior.

Persons I Have Challenged	How I Challenged Them	How Their Behavior Changed

If this brief review of only three situations suggests that your aggressive challenges to others are not resulting in the behavioral changes you expected, then it is time to consider some alternative approaches. Nobody wants you to accept sloppy work from a coworker or tolerate bad behavior from your teenager. But you do need to ask how much sense it makes for a smart, analytical person like you to continue to engage in ineffective strategies. Consider, at least on paper, practicing some alternative methods of responding to your disappointments. For example, if you routinely find errors in the work of a colleague, you may have inadvertently reinforced a toxic pattern of finding and fixing errors for them, making any improvement in their work unnecessary and impossible. The next time you receive work from that person, what can you do before you pick up your red pen and start marking the errors?

We have noticed that clients with this challenge apply a strategy adopted from the world of education called a *rubric* (from the Latin "rule"), or more simply, a *scoring guide.* In clear and precise terms, identify in collaboration with a coworker exactly what represents different levels of performance. For example, a score of "Exemplary" might include the following:

> My document has no errors in fact, grammar, spelling, or format. Before I submitted it to you, I not only thoroughly reviewed it myself but also asked another colleague to check it carefully and I already corrected the errors that we found. I have access to the original sources I used so I know that I can verify the facts in the document at a moment's notice. The format is flawless and matches our organization's style manual. I've taken time to read what you and other senior leaders have written about this subject in the past, so I am certain that this document is consistent with our best practices and prevailing research.

A score of "Close, but Not Finished" might include:

> I reviewed this document—just as I did the last few times—and I think it's accurate. I have almost all of the factual assertions supported with evidence, and most of the evidence is available to me somewhere in the office. The format is the same I used last time. I tried to reflect what I heard you say about this when we discussed the assignment.

A score of "Not Ready" might include:

> This is really just a draft and I have not had time to review it. The content is based more on my memory than on evidence that I have been able to locate. The format is the best I can remember from the papers I wrote in college, and the truth is I haven't seen a copy of the style manual. Since I'm the author of the document, I didn't think I had to consider what you or anyone else had to say about it.

You can make these scoring guides a bit tongue-in-cheek, but they make a serious point. The "I" language means that your colleague is taking ownership of his or her performance. There is no guesswork. The more clear and specific your scoring guide is, the more success you will see in eventual performance. The scoring guide techniques shift the burden from your being a high-priced proofreader and eternal critical of everything around you, to being a leader with a clear vision of what "exemplary" performance really is. We have used this technique for team performance, technology integration, leadership development, financial reviews, and a host of other areas. To be effective, you cannot just buy a book of scoring guides, but you must take the time to generate these collaboratively with your colleagues. The goal is to get them to take ownership of their performance and take you out of the role of being the auditor of other people's work. It's not difficult—we have seen primary school students write scoring guides that are stunningly clear and specific. It is, however, rare. The expectations that people have of one another at work and at home are rarely articulated except in the negative. We are clear and specific about our dissatisfactions, but rarely do we express in detail what would create an "exemplary" state of affairs.

Take a moment to consider something you have found particularly disappointing, a situation in which the performance you expected is almost never what is delivered. How can you take a different approach to this situation? Try creating a scoring guide. First, describe the task or behavior that you intend to address:

____

____

____

____

____

____

____

____

Write three levels of performance in the following table. Give them whatever scores you want—wonderful, wretched, amazing, awful, complete, incomplete—whatever you think could be used with your colleagues in an appropriate way. For each of the three scores, describe in specific detail the attributes of that level of performance.

Performance Level	Attributes of Performance

NEXT STEPS IN THE 100-DAY RENEWAL PROJECT

Think of the specific meetings, conversations, and actions you wish to take in order to improve your reality orientation within the next hundred days. Because you are experimenting with new ideas and behaviors, don't expect them to be instantly successful. The more specific you are, the more likely it is that you will accomplish the task, analyze the result, and use that analysis to improve your performance. Table 9.1 provides some sample steps in a 100-Day Renewal Project that bear directly on reality.

Write down your own action steps in the following table using the LEAD technique introduced in Chapter Six:

What do you need to LEARN?

What EVIDENCE do you need to collect and analyze?

What ATTITUDES and expectations must be developed?

What DECISIONS must be made?

Action Steps	People and Networks Engaged

Table 9.1 Samples of Actions That Will Activate Reality Within This Project

Action Steps	People and Networks Engaged
Collaborate with my team to develop a scoring guide to help us achieve excellence in a specific outcome. Each person can use it to self-assess on a daily basis. The whole team will reflect together on our progress on Tuesdays and Fridays.	Work team
Brainstorm a list of at least twenty descriptors about our organization (team). Start each sentence with the words, "We are known for. . . ." Sort the list into two categories: (1) patterns that work for us and (2) patterns that hold us back. Identify first steps to eliminate patterns that hold you back and first steps to leverage patterns that are helpful. This step could be repeated with customers.	Work team, leaders, and managers could do this as a whole system activity
Identify the "snakes, wasps, and mosquitoes" in your organization. Where do you spend most of your time as a leader? Where do your team members spend most of their time? At what cost to achievement of the organization's most cherished goals?	Systemwide managers and leaders
Schedule a conversation each week with a leader or mentor within or from outside your organization and ask him or her for a different perspective about something about which you hold very strong views.	Colleague or mentor
Plan to have a difficult conversation with an individual or team to focus on strategies to improve a process or outcome.	Plan with my coach

COACHING CONVERSATION

"The past two weeks have had some highs and lows," said Dwight as he began the next coaching conversation.

"What went well for you?" asked the coach.

"Well, I made a list of people I yelled at—actually, I can't even remember them all, but there are enough I do remember that it didn't take long to have a dozen names. Not just coworkers, but a guy at the gas station I didn't even know, my lawyer—even my own sister. Anyway, I apologized. I just said, 'I was a jerk the other day and I'm sorry.' At least my sister said what everybody else was probably thinking, because she said that yes, I was a jerk, and what else was new? But I think at least for a few people it might be the beginning of a better relationship. I certainly noticed that a few of them said hello to me rather than avoiding me, which I guess has been the normal routine around here."

"That's great," replied the coach. "You said that there were some lows. Tell me about those."

"Well, Fred was late—again—on his weekly report. He does this every week, and every week I yell at him about it. When he does turn it in, it always has an error—it's like he's baiting me and wondering if I can find it. So, I've been this nice guy for two weeks—well, maybe not nice, but at least I've tried very hard not to be a jerk. I was demanding, didn't yell, didn't ask obnoxious questions. So what does Fred do? He's late again. Maybe this approach just doesn't work with him."

"Aside from not yelling at him, what else did you change with regard to your approach to Fred?" A long silence followed this question from the coach.

"Well—nothing," Dwight said. "I didn't do anything different from what I've done for the past six months, and I guess I shouldn't be surprised that Fred keeps doing the same thing. But he's a grown-up. He's got a college degree. I shouldn't have to spell it out for him."

"Why don't you and Fred sit down together and achieve clarity on your expectations?" asked the coach. "Right now he appears to have concluded that your expectations are either impossible or mysterious, so he doesn't try meeting them. Would you be willing to create a scoring guide with Fred so that you both know what to expect?"

"I read about that, but if it's used for primary school students, I really don't see how it's appropriate for use in an office. He's likely to be insulted by it, and I guess I am not wild about the idea either. This is work and it's time to put the crayons away."

"You're quite right that this technique is used with children. It's also used in organizations with billion-dollar budgets and thousands of employees."

"Does it really work?" asked Dwight.

"Not always—certainly not on the first draft. People usually realize that they had many implicit expectations for high performance that had never been made explicit. Almost always people say they wish they'd had this level of clarity months or years earlier. But you and Fred will be the judges of that. Let me know in a couple of weeks how it's going."

Coaching conversations do not work miracles or provide mystical insights. But when conducted effectively, they help clients approach reality in a healthy and balanced way. The cynic may not lose a pervasive sense of mistrust, but he might admit that cynicism is not an effective strategy. The gullible person might continue to give a trusting ear to untrustworthy sources, but she might also begin asking questions and taking personal responsibility for the consequences of gullibility. The question for reality is a process, not an event, and the pursuit of it will influence almost every interaction you have in your waking hours. It is worth the effort and it will help you succeed in the other elements of the Renewal Coaching framework.

CHAPTER 10

Reciprocity
Coaching in Harmony

In his famous *Treatise on Harmony*, published in 1722, French composer Jean-Philippe Rameau (1971) lamented that the contemporary music of his time had caused people to become less interested in the principles of musical harmony. "One might say that reason has lost its rights, while experience has acquired a certain authority" (p. xxxiii). But Rameau warns us that "conclusions drawn from experience are often false, or at least leave us with doubts that only reason can dispel" (p. xxxiii). In the context of Renewal Coaching, "harmony" does not imply pleasant music, such as Rameau himself composed. It rather refers to the more profound challenge that Rameau has issued—that we not accept the limits of our own experience but seek to learn about the experience of others in pursuit of broader understanding.

If you find such efforts challenging, you are not alone. Jean-Jacques Rousseau was the philosopher who gave us the "Social Contract." A true Renaissance man, his many gifts included not only philosophy but also music, law, theater, and diplomacy. He studied Rameau's work and found it profoundly difficult. Perhaps it hit too close to home in that Rameau insists there is a social contract of sorts between composer and musician, with each having responsibilities to the other. He provides detailed instructions as well to accompanists, noting the reciprocal obligations between soloists, choristers, and accompanists. In this chapter, you will consider the mutual obligations not only of coach and client, but also of other stakeholders with whom you interact. When reciprocity is unbalanced, either by giving too much or too little of yourself, then relationships are damaged and personal contentment is elusive. Coaches in particular are subject to the imbalance of giving too much, seeking to "satisfy" clients not through the performance of their coaching duties but by submitting to demands that are unreasonable and inappropriate. People in helping professions, such as social work, health care, and education, can also achieve the worst of both worlds, in which they neither satisfy others to whom they are giving too much nor satisfy their own desire to be seen as a worthy helper. When we give too little, we are like the person who tries to perform the concerto without an orchestra. Regardless of how gifted the performer may be, there will be long periods of silence when the orchestra should be playing, and the musical effect of the soloist is not remotely close to the combined impact of all of the musicians together.

Reciprocity Assessment Review

Take a moment to review your Reciprocity Assessment from Chapter Four. If you have not yet taken the assessment, please do so by logging on to www.RenewalCoaching.com and selecting Assessments.

My Reciprocity Assessment score: ____________________

Key insights from my responses to the open-ended questions in the Reciprocity Assessment:

____

____

____

____

____

RENEWAL MOMENTS

Karen and Cheryl are partners in an enterprise whose creativity, service, and community image are legendary. Karen, a scientist by training, developed a process for recycling plastic waste into inexpensive and very strong building materials. Cheryl, an MBA and former manager at a Fortune 500 company, knew that Karen had a winning idea if only it could be marketed effectively. Together they have built a fast-growing company that has been featured in a popular business magazine as one of the five hundred fastest-growing companies in the United States for three consecutive years. Their eighty employees enjoy attractive benefits and they have received national recognition for being a family-friendly company. Karen's environmental activism led her to explore how to recycle plastic waste in the first place, and she ensures that her company is at the forefront of environmental responsibility. She is also on many boards and a well-known advocate for social justice in her community and, to a growing degree, on the national scale.

Behind the scenes, however, the relationship between Karen and Cheryl, equal partners in the business, is enduring enormous stress. Because this stress is affecting their friendship, their employees, their customers, and their business, they have sought the support of a professional coach. Although both partners have two small children at home, their support structures are dramatically different. Karen's husband took a leave from work and stays home with the children while Karen is at the office or on one of her increasingly frequent trips for board meetings of nonprofit organizations in which she is active. Although Karen is proud of the business and appreciates the work that Cheryl has done, she finds it boring. She likes the financial independence that, after years of sacrifice and low income, she now enjoys, but she doesn't appreciate Cheryl's expectation that she spend time on budgets, plans, and people issues. "That's not my department," is one of Karen's favorite statements.

Cheryl's marriage broke up while she was building the business, and although she can afford top-notch day care and a bevy of evening babysitters to cover the many long nights at the office, she is clearly exhausted. She has no time for the kids, has not been on a date in two years, and is feeling frustrated and angry at having to do the work of two executives while Karen's public appearances lead most people to believe that Karen, not Cheryl, is running the company. Privately, Cheryl seethes with anger. She has even screamed about it—but only when completely alone in the car and safely out of earshot of anyone. Cheryl is known at work as someone who will always help, but not always wisely. Her attempt to "help" at the loading dock ended disastrously when she wrenched her back and the foreman had to tell her politely but firmly that it was not safe for her to try to do things she did not know how to do. She has personally lent money to family members and employees with no prospect of getting it back, and her last vacation was an extravagant trip she had attempted with her husband in order to save the marriage. That trip, like the marriage, ended badly, and it appears to have soured her on leisure travel.

Karen has suspected that Cheryl is not happy, but she has also assumed that Cheryl is doing what she wants. In fact, while Karen likes the money, she resents some of the ways in which she has made it. "I can't believe we're taking money from the Department of Defense!" Karen said, only half-jokingly. "That's not going to help my image with my antiwar friends at my next board meeting."

"That contract is part of what pays for you to ride in first class when you go to that meeting," Cheryl replied coldly.

"What are you so uptight about? You're rich, single, and independent—doing what you've always wanted to do. You're the luckiest girl in the world," Karen said, laughing a bit nervously as she left the office for her most recent trip.

"Right," Cheryl replied flatly, confident that Karen had no idea how hurtful and insensitive her comment was. "Lucky girl, that's me."

Do the interactions between Karen and Cheryl bring to mind relationships in your life? Take a few minutes to identify one such relationship and describe the parts of it that are not reciprocal:

____

____

____

____

____

IF RECIPROCITY IS A STRENGTH

If you scored between 41 and 70 on the Reciprocity Assessment, you are among the rare people for whom reciprocity is a strength. You can capitalize on this strength by continuing to be a model for your colleagues and family members. You give, but within boundaries. You can decline a request without feeling that you have let down the whole world. You can safeguard time and resources for yourself without feeling covetous. At the same time, you don't have any trouble recalling the last time you helped a neighbor, friend, or coworker—that sort of assistance comes naturally too. At the same time, you know when to stay in the background and your help is never intrusive.

Although this strength is a genuine asset for you at home and at work, there is a cautionary note in all of this applause. You may think that other people tend to be like you; therefore you can be surprised and upset by people who are not. You can be contemptuous of the takers and the givers, thinking that the former have no conscience and the latter have no responsibility. But they are just imperfect people like you, and they might have other strengths from which you can learn.

Most of all, value your reciprocal relationships. They are rare and should be treasured and nurtured.

Think of three relationships, including at least one that is personal and one that is professional, that are genuinely reciprocal. Then, in the following table, write down a simple way you can nurture these relationships today.

Reciprocal Relationship	Ways I Can Nurture This Relationship

IF RECIPROCITY IS A WEAKNESS

About the last thing you need in your life is more criticism. If you scored high on the Reciprocity Assessment, you have already beaten yourself up for more mistakes than you can count. You certainly do not hear the appreciation of others, because it is tinged with an echo of reproach from inside your own head. If you scored low on the assessment, you are weary of the complaints of other people who do not know your background and experiences. You are not this way because you are an insensitive and acquisitive demon, any more than the high-scorer is an irresponsible doormat, though both of you may frame these scores in such extreme terms. In fact, you are a product of your experiences, and they create the analytical framework within which you perceive every event. For low-scoring individuals, perhaps you have been taken advantage of in the past and have resolved never to let it occur again. Thus you shut out those around you and always maintain the power in every relationship. For high-scorers, perhaps you grew up being expected to care for others and you never stopped. Even though your younger siblings are in their twenties, you continue to treat them as dependent on you. You do this not out of gullibility or stupidity but because that is what your experiences have led you to expect of yourself. If you were not a caretaker, you would not be a complete person.

What are some experiences from the past that you think might influence your present level of reciprocity?

____

____

____

In the following table, identify some nonreciprocal relationships and identify one part of each relationship—just one—in which a relatively simple change could lead to reciprocity. For example:

> "In almost every meeting we have been in together you have always answered questions that were directed toward me and explained research I conducted as if it were your own. I would like you to allow me to respond to these questions and to agree that you will not explain things for me unless I have made an error that must be publicly and immediately corrected."
>
> "I make the bed seven days a week; I would like you to start making the bed on Friday, Saturday, and Sunday."

"I don't know anything about our finances because I don't balance the checkbook. I would like to have a discussion once a month about how much money we have and where it is."

"I've taken control and planned our last three trips. I would like for you to take this responsibility for the next trip."

Relationship	Change That Could Lead to Reciprocity

NEXT STEPS IN THE 100-DAY RENEWAL PROJECT

Identify action steps inspired by your reflections in this chapter as well as by your assessment results. The more specific your action steps are, the more likely it is that you will attain them. It is important to remember that the roots of nonreciprocal behavior are deep, and changes will be incremental. It is essential that you not only attempt to improve reciprocity in work and in personal relationships, but also that you identify and nurture those few relationships that are reciprocal. Table 10.1 provides some sample steps in a 100-Day Renewal Project that bear directly on reciprocity.

After reviewing the samples in Table 10.1, write down your own action steps in the following table using the LEAD technique introduced in Chapter Six:

What do you need to LEARN?

What EVIDENCE do you need to collect and analyze?

Table 10.1 Samples of Actions That Will Activate Reciprocity Within This Project

Action Steps	People and Networks Engaged
What promises to others are languishing on your plate? Examine what is stopping you from following through. Decide what you will do, then communicate this information to the other person or group.	People affected by your lack of follow-though
Identify information or results you require from someone else. Make the request, being certain to be specific about what you are asking for. Provide a deadline.	Colleague, family member, team
In your current project, identify something in which you are not an expert. Develop a learning plan that includes increasing your own knowledge as well as seeking out the expertise of others.	Team
Look at your closest business and personal relationships and honestly assess your contribution to mutually important projects. Do you give as much as you take? Do you receive well? What would transform any imbalance?	Reflection with coach or trusted friend or colleague
Plan the week ahead with attention to reciprocity. Decide to remove some things from your calendar and schedule other events accordingly.	

What ATTITUDES and expectations must be developed?
What DECISIONS must be made?

Action Steps	People and Networks Engaged

Action Steps	People and Networks Engaged

COACHING CONVERSATION

Not every coaching conversation results in behavioral change and a happily-ever-after ending. After three months of intensive coaching, Karen and Cheryl agreed that their lives were taking very different turns. They had enjoyed a successful partnership and built a wonderful business, but they could both see that they were not willing to create a reciprocal relationship. They had been approached by other companies in the past for a possible acquisition, and they had always declined because they enjoyed the independence of running their own organization. Now, however, it was clear that both of them needed a break. They had seen entrepreneurial friends create great companies and then lose everything because they did not sell when they had the opportunity. Cheryl and Karen decided that they had worked too hard to take such a risk, so they took a reasonable offer that gave them both financial independence, and parted ways. Coaches do not create or restore reciprocity. They ask good questions and provide accurate feedback. In this case, the coaches did their job well, though the results were not what they had expected. They did, however, help both of these enterprising women achieve insights that will guide them in their future ventures.

CHAPTER 11

Resilience
Coaching Through Pain

Resilience is the ability to bounce back from painful experiences with a transformed perspective. Resilient people do not have fewer disappointments than the rest of us, but they react to pain in a strikingly different way. These people are not naive optimists and the pain they endure is real, often deeply tragic. But they endure and they ultimately bounce back.

There are three prominent features of resilient behavior. First, resilient people interpret information differently than others. Criticism or silence from a colleague or romantic partner may be disturbing, but it is neither a threat to their professional standing nor a dagger in their hearts. They accept experience as a piece of data, not as an infallible predictor of the future. Second, they have a sense of personal efficacy and empowerment. Although they are not delusionary about their powers, they do not surrender themselves to the whims of fate. Third, they take appropriate responsibility for their role in unfortunate events without becoming compulsively and excessively responsible for everything. If they have an accident in a blizzard, they accept responsibility for driving in bad weather, driving too fast for the weather conditions, or purchasing a car that did not handle well in predictable weather. They are not, however, responsible for provoking other drivers to behave badly or for enticing Zeus, the god of sky and weather, to send the blizzard from the heavens.

Public examples of resilience can be intimidating. In the past decade, from the heroes of 9/11 to the countless models of resilience in soldiers, nurses, teachers, and many others, we see visible evidence of people who respond to devastating injuries and personal loss with hope, optimism, and determination. Every generation offers similar extraordinary models. Although inspiring, those models can also send the message that resilience is limited to the exceptional few, and that the tragedies associated with resilience must be profound, visible, and life-altering. In fact, resilience is essential to renewal for all of us, whether the context is the battlefield or the living room. The loss of a job, betrayal of a loved one, or rejection by a colleague or friend can lead us into a tailspin if we are not equipped with resilience.

Organizational resilience depends on the personal resilience of each person within the system, especially the leaders. People observe top managers and executives within the organization for their response to dilemmas, downturns, and unexpected results. Do leaders encourage innovation in the face of adversity or do they shut down new ideas? Do they see opportunity in adversity or do they judge, blame, and fire the person or persons they see as at the root of the "mistake"? Do they transmit fear or even cowardice to those around them? Do they deny the reality of the adversity and then go on to make decisions that are not appropriate to the situation? Leaders of organizations facing adversity are only as resilient as they are in their personal lives. Especially during times of rapid change in technology, economics, political upheaval, and even natural disasters, resilience is an essential business strategy. Profitable and successful organizations expect, support, and reward resilience from each individual within the organization.

Resilience Assessment Review

Take a moment to review your Resilience Assessment. If you have not yet taken the assessment, please do so by logging on to www.RenewalCoaching.com and selecting Assessments.

My Resilience Assessment score: ____________________

Key insights from my responses to the open-ended questions in the Resilience Assessment:

____

____

____

RENEWAL MOMENTS

Marco and Maria were childhood sweethearts who worked their way through college. They planned a life that would be far more successful than their parents had enjoyed, and they executed their plan well. They both put their education to work with the local electrical utility—Marco in the accounting department and Maria in engineering. They worked hard and were successful, turning down occasional job offers elsewhere in order to provide a stable home for their family that eventually included three children and a variety of pets. Although their parents had led a nomadic existence, searching for available work, Marco and Maria craved, above all, stability for their family. Now both forty-five, they were within sight of taking early retirement when their employer was acquired by another corporation two years ago. Because both of them participated in the company's stock ownership plan, both benefitted from the takeover, at least according to the balances in their accounts. They eagerly transferred their balances to shares in the new company and cooperated with the new owners, even though it was quite clear from the day the acquisition was announced that the corporate parent was strongly focused on cutting costs. Because of their seniority and experience, they imagined that they were exempt from any job cuts and continued to do what they had always done—work hard to provide a secure and stable environment for their family.

Precisely four weeks after the Friday on which the acquisition was completed, Marco and Maris, along with about forty other employees, were called into a conference room that seated only about half that number. "I'm sorry it's so uncomfortable in here," an executive they did not recognize began. She was elegantly dressed and confident in manner, but clearly uncomfortable in this setting. "My name is Marjorie Jenkins and I'm with the outplacement firm retained by this company to assist you in your transition. I'm sorry to say that my first duty is to tell you that your positions have been eliminated, effective immediately. We want to handle this in as compassionate a way as possible, so we will be providing you with information on severance packages in the mail to your home address. For now, however, I need to ask you to give your badges and entry cards to the gentlemen at the door who will escort you to the parking lot. Any personal items that you left in the office will be sent to you. I'm sorry, but we cannot allow you to return to your offices at this time and we need to ask that you proceed immediately to the parking lot."

Walking to the parking lot in a daze, Maria and Marco shared the ride home in silence. They had one child who was a junior in college and although they had saved diligently since she was born, Theresa's college fund was exhausted after her first two years at a very expensive school. The other two kids were in high school, with college just a couple of years away. A proud homeowner, Marco maintained their meticulous lawn and Maria clearly enjoyed being the host of her extended family. She and Marco were the successful ones, the only ones from her family to graduate from college and own homes. She relished her status as an engineer in a field that did not include many women, particularly when she had started twenty years ago. When she spoke to high school girls about the opportunities for women in engineering and science, she felt enormous pride and hoped that several of her nieces would follow in her footsteps. In the recession of 2008, Maria and Marco were hardly alone, and they knew other people, including several in their own family, who had lost jobs. They simply never expected this to happen to them. "We did everything right," said Maria. "This just isn't fair." She rarely lost her composure and was not going to at this point, at least on the outside. But as she sat in the car in the garage she simply said, "It's all over" as visions of catastrophe filled her head. "The house, college for the kids, our lives—it's just over."

"Wait," Marco said. "We have three healthy kids. I'm married to the best woman in the world. We have more than our parents ever dreamed about." "Had," interrupted Maria. "We had, until an hour ago, more than our parents ever dreamed of, and now I'm just like them—broke and resentful and bitter."

"You're the smartest woman I know—an engineer! You're going to do fine," started Marco, but before he finished his thought, Maria got out of the car and walked silently into the house. Marco knew from experience to leave Maria alone. When she was not selected for promotion several years ago, she spent months in a state of deep anger, resenting not only the managers who made the decision, but also her choice of career, her professors, her colleagues, and it seemed even Marco. When Theresa was diagnosed with a learning disability, Maria despaired that Theresa's hopes for college were finished, but Marco spent an hour every evening with Theresa, patiently working through lessons that helped her organize her ideas in a graphic format that she could better understand. Although Marco would never wish for a learning disability for any child, he admitted to himself that he looked forward to his time with Theresa, time that he knew very few teenage kids were willing to spend with any parent. He beamed when Theresa graduated from high school with honors and excelled in college, applying systematic ways of looking at information that students without her disability had never learned.

Now, Marco knew the obvious: that his accounting skills were not unique and that he could be replaced—perhaps he already had been—by someone half his age who had better technology skills and demanded half his salary. But he thought of his grandparents who had left Honduras as teenagers to come to this country illegally so that their children would be, as he often said, "real Americans." Papa was the real American, thought Marco, recalling how proudly his grandfather flew the American flag on every holiday while his son, Marco's father, had been indifferent about the blessings of being born in America. "This? It's nothing compared to what Pap had to face," Marco thought, as he walked into the kitchen.

Maria and Marco have both faced the same loss, but their reactions are strikingly different. Undoubtedly you know someone who has suffered loss at work or at home. Perhaps you have as well. Take a moment to describe your reactions to this scenario.

When I think about Maria, I think about . . .

____

____

____

____

____

When I think about Marco, I think about . . .

____

____

____

____

____

Just as Maria and Marco responded differently to the same event, your response will no doubt vary widely from that of others, depending on your perspective. Perhaps you think Marco is delusionary. "I don't care if he flies the flag on top of the Statue of Liberty, that's not going to pay for his daughter's college bills." Perhaps you admire him but find more sympathy than empathy. "It was a great immigrant story, and too bad it didn't have a happy ending. That's life, and the sooner Marco figures it out, the better."

Whatever your reaction, take a moment to reframe your initial perception of Maria and Marco, this time with regard to the three lenses of resilience: analysis of information, personal empowerment, and appropriate responsibility. For each resilience characteristic, challenge yourself to see a completely opposite perspective. Write your reframed perspectives in the following table.

Resilience Characteristic	Maria	Marco
Analysis of information		
Personal empowerment		
Appropriate responsibility		

IF RESILIENCE IS A STRENGTH

If you scored between 0 and 25, you are among a group of people for whom resilience is a strength. Your reaction to disappointment is nothing short of astounding. You don't just bounce back from disappointment, but you jump back, surprising family, friends, and colleagues with your ability to endure in the face of difficulty. In fact, you are so resilient that others may see you as arrogant and cocky. They may psychoanalyze you behind your back—"She's not really resilient," they will theorize, "she just keeps it all bottled up inside. Just watch—some day she's going to have a meltdown." Confident and successful people like you will always have your share of critics, and it is to your great credit that you do not take their criticism personally. Although you respect feedback from others, ill-tempered and mindless criticism is just noise—that's what insecure people do, and you're actually a bit sorry for them.

To capitalize on this strength, you should seek challenging opportunities where the risk of failure is evident but controllable. In business or nonprofit work, this could be a turnaround of a troubled organization. In your personal life, it might be helping a child or friend who appears to alienate others. You enjoy these challenges, and if you do not succeed, you know that you will learn many valuable insights for the future. Your appetite for challenge can lead to overcommitment, to embracing impossible deadlines, tasks, or relationships. Just because resilience is a strength, you need not demonstrate it all the time. You might be overdue for some time for yourself. This doesn't mean a vacation, which might be, for you, more arduous than work. It does mean some time for self-care, reflection, and quiet—perhaps a walk, a concert, or dinner with a friend. Slow down. You have a great deal to contribute to the world right now, and the rest of us need you to be healthy.

Please take a moment and record here some ways that you can nurture your strength in resilience:

____

____

____

IF RESILIENCE IS A WEAKNESS

The world faces extraordinary challenges—wars, recession, wholesale destruction of economic value—and the toll taken on the lives of people around the world is profound and perhaps permanent. People don't need inspirational pep talks; they need hope and action. If you want to change the way you respond to loss, you need to take some practical steps to make hope a reality rather than an illusion. Part of accepting hope as a reality is accepting loss as a reality. Your loss is real and possibly enormous, but it is not total if you have the sentience to read this and the breath to discuss it with a trusted friend. As you confront your most important losses, describe them with precision, neither minimizing them nor exaggerating them. Then consider how you can apply the principles of resilience—analysis, empowerment, and responsibility. Start with your present reaction, then try to reframe it using a different approach. Consider the following example:

Loss: My department was eliminated and I lost my job.

Present Framework:

Analysis: I lost not only my job but also my self-respect, the respect of my colleagues, and my hopes for the future. I'll never get another job.

Empowerment: It doesn't make any difference what I do. The jobs are all going to other countries, employers are prejudiced against middle-aged people like me, and I can't learn any new skills.

Responsibility: If only I had listened to my mother and gone into medicine, I'd still have a job. It's all my fault and I deserved it; it's a just punishment for me not listening to Mom.

Alternative Framework:

Analysis: I lost my job, but I'm the same person I was the day before and I'll be the same person the day after. I'm a decent and honest person and I've accomplished a lot in my life. Losing a job is really awful, but I have family, friends, and a personal level of strength that will get me through this.

Empowerment: I can take some specific actions to market myself more effectively in what is a really competitive market right now. In just a few months I can become certified in a new software program that will make me competitive with the newest college graduates. That way I'll have the technical skills of young people and the maturity and experience I've acquired over the years. I can also make a list of every colleague I've had in the past several years—there must be easily twenty or thirty people in many different companies. I'll call five of them every day and start building a network.

Responsibility: I certainly chose my line of work and went to work for my former employer voluntarily. But neither the economic crisis nor the management decisions the company made that led them into trouble are my fault. I was happy to take credit when things were going well, so I'll take some responsibility now. But bad things happen to a lot of good people, and I know I didn't deserve this. I'm basically a good person and I'm going to bounce back from this. I deserve to.

BUILDING RESILIENCE THROUGH H.O.P.E.

Our work with clients around the world has included senior executives of large organizations and leaders in impoverished parts of Africa and Asia, but regardless of the cultural or economic context, we have observed that hope in isolation is not an effective strategy. Rather, such a strategy is a combination of factors that includes hope, optimism, purpose, and empathy: H.O.P.E.

Hope, the feeling that things will get better, has many definitions. One of my favorites is "to look forward to with desire and reasonable confidence" (Random House, 1987). This definition conveys neither the naivete of a mere feeling unsupported by analysis nor the artificiality of a wish. Hope, along with confidence, can be real and reasonable.

Optimism also is not a feeling but an observation. We have reason to be optimistic about economic matters not because recession and unemployment are illusions but because the world has a long and extensively documented history of economic recovery following every economic collapse.

Purpose is similarly an objective phenomenon, not the result of an evanescent inspiration. People—whether family members, friends, and colleagues today or people we have not yet met—depend on us. Although you may have a deeply theological purpose for your life, you also have a practical purpose today, right now. Doug's mother, entering her ninth decade of life with two artificial hips and failing eyes, has a remarkable sense of purpose; she teaches, writes, researches, and volunteers every day. She does not completely understand why people half her age and in much better physical condition do not also bound out of bed every morning with at least an equal sense of purpose.

Empathy is the ability to understand the challenges of others. We understand our own difficulties better when we seek to understand the pain of others.

Understanding H.O.P.E.

Each element of H.O.P.E. can be assessed and placed on a matrix to provide a better understanding of your own level of resilience. First, evaluate your level of agreement with each of the following belief statements associated with hope, optimism, purpose, and empathy.

H.O.P.E. Inventory: Hope, Optimism, Purpose, Empathy

H.O.P.E. Characteristics	Strongly Disagree Uncertain Strongly Agree
Hope: I believe that my best days are in the future, not in the past.	1 2 3 4 5 6 7 8 9 10 11 12 13 14 15 16 17 18 19 20 21 22 23 24 25
Optimism: I believe that things are generally getting better for me and for most of the people I care about.	1 2 3 4 5 6 7 8 9 10 11 12 13 14 15 16 17 18 19 20 21 22 23 24 25
Purpose: I have a reason to get up every day. People count on me, and even though I don't always do the greatest work, I know that other people really need me and depend on me.	1 2 3 4 5 6 7 8 9 10 11 12 13 14 15 16 17 18 19 20 21 22 23 24 25
Empathy: When I see someone in real pain—whether emotional, physical, mental, or other—it affects me deeply and I want to help them.	1 2 3 4 5 6 7 8 9 10 11 12 13 14 15 16 17 18 19 20 21 22 23 24 25

Hope + Optimism Score: ________________ Purpose + Empathy Score: ________________

Total Score: ________________

In order to have confidence that your ratings are accurate, take a moment to provide, in the following table, evidence, examples, or interactions that support and explain your rating. If this exercise leads you to revise your level of agreement with each belief statement, please make those revisions now.

Understanding H.O.P.E. (continued)

H.O.P.E. Indicator	My Rating	Evidence, Examples, or Interactions
Hope		
Optimism		
Purpose		
Empathy		

Use your analysis to place your scores on the H.O.P.E. matrix in Figure 11.1. Your personal H.O.P.E. assessment depends on the intersection of your H.O.P.E. scores. Write your Hope and Optimism score on the vertical axis and your Purpose and Empathy score on the horizontal axis. For example, if your Hope and Optimism score is 20, mark the vertical axis at 20; and if your Purpose and Empathy score is 80, mark the horizontal axis at 80. This will place the intersection of the two points in the lower right-hand quadrant. Read the rest of the chapter to learn more about what these scores mean for you.

As the H.O.P.E. matrix suggests, low scores on every level reflect despair and depression. Without any of the elements of H.O.P.E., one can conclude that life lacks meaning and the future is bleak. Driven by a strong sense of purpose and possessing deep empathy for others, one may nevertheless lack hope and optimism. This may describe Marco at the moment, because his despair over his job does not overwhelm his deep sense of purpose as

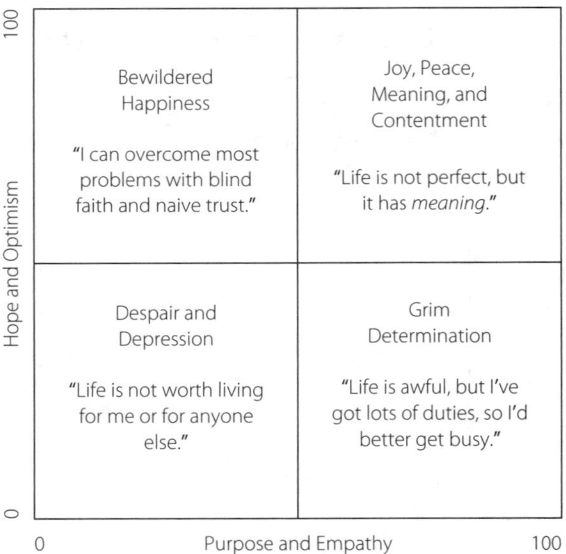

Figure 11.1 H.O.P.E.

a father, spouse, and citizen. This quadrant, labeled "grim determination," may not be sustainable in the long term, but it is a far more constructive place to be than despair. As a practical matter, this means that people who have suffered deep loss may benefit in the short term from seeking to help others. When you have lost a job or a loved one, volunteer service may not be the first thing that comes to mine. People who have lost a life partner or their life's work may not feel a great deal of hope, but they can nevertheless have an objective sense of purpose.

In the upper left-hand quadrant of the matrix are those who have high levels of optimism and hope but have not found a deep sense of purpose or a strong sense of empathy for others in pain. They exhibit a childlike faith that things will get better, but underneath their naive and unsustainable beliefs there is fragility. These are people who will pay $300 they do not have for an inspirational video or join a throng in a stadium to listen to shallow exhortations but not translate their inspiration into action. Equipped with all four elements—hope, optimism, purpose, and empathy—we have the opportunity to experience peace and contentment, and perhaps even that elusive feeling of joy. Most people are in transition from one quadrant to another. H.O.P.E. is a process and a journey, not a permanent state of affairs. Life is full of setbacks, and with each passing year there are more opportunities for both fulfillment and disappointment. Thus we traverse these quadrants many times, building resilience with each experience.

NEXT STEPS IN THE 100-DAY RENEWAL PROJECT

Identify specific action steps inspired by your reflections in this chapter. The more specific your tasks are, the more likely it is that you will accomplish these tasks within the next hundred days. Pay particular attention to losses that are affecting you right now, and consider specific ways that you can reframe your understanding of that loss with an alternative analysis, a sense of empowerment, and a clear but appropriate degree of personal responsibility. Consider specific steps that you can take that will provide a sense of purpose and build your empathy for the losses suffered by others. Table 11.1 provides some sample steps in a 100-Day Renewal Project that bear directly on resilience.

After reviewing the samples in Table 11.1, write down your own action steps in the following table. You may also return to the 100-Day Renewal

Table 11.1 Samples of Actions That Will Activate Resilience Within This Project

Action Steps	People and Networks Engaged
Review your last three projects. What went as planned? What did not go as planned? How did you respond? How did you lead your team to respond? What are the top takeaways for the current project?	Colleagues
Evaluate the status of your current project and communicate your impressions to the team. Compare progress to milestones expected by this point. Together develop steps to break through the current challenges.	Work team, leaders, managers
Become involved in networks and professional organizations that specialize in the topics relevant to your project. Contribute ideas and be open to learning.	Networks, professional associations, mentors
Identify opportunities out of every setback. Think out of the box by finishing this sentence: Now that ____________ is the current reality, ____________ is a new possibility. Answer this ten to twenty times, first by yourself and then with others invested in the project.	Colleagues, family members
Reevaluate the appropriateness of your strategies given the current reality. Revise or refine them.	Colleagues

Project template we introduced in Chapter Six and enter your actions there. Be sure to use the LEAD technique:

What do you need to LEARN?
What EVIDENCE do you need to collect and analyze?
What ATTITUDES and expectations must be developed?
What DECISIONS must be made?

Action Steps	People and Networks Engaged

Action Steps	People and Networks Engaged

COACHING CONVERSATION

Maria and Marco were fortunate to find support from a coaching organization that provided 10 percent of their services for free or at reduced rates to people of limited economic means. This coaching organization had a particular outreach to executives who had been laid off and provided the same level of professionalism and service as they would if these executives had retained their leadership positions. This turned out to be more than a contribution to the greater good by these coaches; it was also a smart strategy for their professional practice. As their clients returned to the workforce, they were so impressed by the services provided by the coaches that they retained them in their new positions.

In the weeks after their exit from the utility company that had returned their years of service with an abrupt and ungrateful departure, Maria and Marco mourned their losses—not only financial, but also the loss of associations, daily meaning, and contact with friends of long standing. For Maria, the losses were deeply personal and pervasive, and she was haunted by a sense of worthlessness. Although Marco's external appearance continued to exude confidence and optimism, he too was deeply affected by the losses, feeling that he was required to be the strong man of the family. He did not understand that far from finding this endearing, Maria found it inauthentic and infuriating. Their coaches helped Maria and Marco to express their reactions to their losses with clarity and specificity. Each time Maria would start to engage in catastrophic thinking, the coach would ask questions that led her to restate her conclusions in a factual way, neither minimizing nor exaggerating her losses. When Marco would drift into blind faith rather than reasoned optimism, his coach would ask him to identify specific steps that he could take to translate his feelings into action.

Maria's resilience breakthrough came the day her coach encouraged (insisted might be a better word) her to keep an appointment with the same urban high school where for more than a decade she had been a regular speaker and inspiration to girls who might consider engineering as a career. "I can't go," Maria protested. "They'll think I'm a phony. They'll ask what makes me so smart if I'm unemployed. They'll know that college sure didn't do me any good."

"You've spoken to teens for many years," the coach replied. "Have you ever seen them exhibit this sort of disrespectful behavior toward you?"

"No," Maria said softly. "They are actually in awe of me. They see my business suit, they hear that I'm an engineer, and they know what responsibilities I've had, and they seem very attentive. The teachers say that these kids are never as quiet and respectful as when I come to class."

"Do you think that's just because of your suit and your job?" asked the coach.

"No, they know I'm for real. Kids know a phony right away, and they know I've had to work hard. They can tell that things did not come easily to me." Maria clearly enjoyed these encounters and was beginning to think that these meetings with teenagers were yet another loss she had not yet mourned.

"Have any of your accomplishments in college or on the job changed?"

"Of course!" snapped Maria. "I lost my job!"

"I understand, but did you lose your college diploma?"

"No, of course not," Maria replied.

"Did you lose any of the promotions and accolades you've had in the past twenty years?"

"Those things already happened—of course I didn't lose them," said Maria, a little less abruptly.

"Did you stop being an honest, decent, and caring person on the day you lost your job? Did you stop being a good engineer?" the coach persisted.

"No. I'm still the same person—the same college graduate, friend, teammate, and engineer I was a year ago."

"Just one more question," the coach continued. "Do you think that the young women in this high school might know something about disappointment and loss and that you could have something even more important to say this year than you ever have in the past?"

Maria, rarely emotional, clenched her jaw and tried to stop her voice from quaking. "I was one of those girls not so many years ago. I know they need me. They need to talk with an adult who is not only successful but also real. They have seen friends and siblings killed in gangs, become addicted to drugs, go to jail, and leave school. They know a lot more about loss than I do. But they don't know very much about how to deal with loss. Maybe I have something I can share with them."

Just as loss is an integral part of life, resilience is an essential part of the Renewal Coaching framework. Without the risks that lead to loss, there would be none of the joys and satisfactions of learning and loving. Without resilience, there can be no renewal.

CHAPTER 12

Resonance
Coaching with Emotional Intelligence

Resonant people ignite others with a sense of hope, optimism, commitment, and joy. Resonant leaders have the ability to inspire others and accomplish even difficult goals with an attitude of goodwill and uncommon passion for outcomes and process. These resonant individuals possess a healthy dose of emotional intelligence, specifically the competencies of self-awareness, self-management, social awareness, and relationship management (Goleman, Boyatzis, & McKee, 2002). Resonance cannot be left to chance; it must be nurtured and replenished. Leaders who do not attend to renewal become fatigued, depleted, and negative, and because of this they create havoc and dissonance in their environment. Nevertheless, people who have learned to sustain resonance realize that emotions are contagious and that a resonant workplace creates a ripe climate for innovation, problem solving, and meaningful work. These leaders know that resonance can make or break momentum for themselves and others, and they reframe their own feelings of frustration, fear, and worry, which are poisonous to renewal and thoughts of the greater good. Leaders who coach and coaches of leaders must resonate with hope, optimism, and goodwill in every interaction because they are in positions of power and emotional influence and can therefore determine how other people feel and what they accomplish.

Resonance Assessment Review

Take a moment to review your Resonance Assessment from Chapter Four. If you have not yet taken the assessment, please do so by logging on to www.RenewalCoaching.com and selecting Assessments.

My Resonance Assessment score: ____________________

Key insights from my responses to the open-ended questions in the Resonance Assessment:

____

____

____

____

____

RESONANCE MOMENTS

Jane is an entrepreneur who works as an independent consultant to law firms. Over the past six years she has developed an excellent reputation with clients and often provides additional services at no cost. She prides herself on going the extra mile and providing strong support during and after every consulting engagement. She loves the work not only because it allows her to earn a good living, but also because she finds the work meaningful. Some of the law firms with which she works are large national firms with offices in several different cities. Although they typically represent large corporations, these firms also provide free legal representation to victims of domestic abuse, a cause to which Jane is deeply committed. When Jane works on a project for these firms, she feels their shared sense of commitment to serving people in need.

Despite her generally positive relationships with clients, there are times, however, when Jane's work is not appreciated. She finds this particularly galling when she offers extra services free of charge and receives criticism rather than praise. The most recent example of this occurred when Jane was providing training for staff members in locations around the country using computer-supported conference technology. This format saved the firm tens of thousands of dollars in travel costs, and Jane's expertise had been generally reliable, but this particular presentation was a challenge from the moment it began. The sound controls were not working properly, so some people who were supposed to speak could not be heard. Because it is so difficult to schedule people in different law offices to participate on the same call at the same time, Jane knew she had to proceed on schedule and try to fix the problem while she was speaking. It was a hectic and stressful experience but, with persistence and a little luck, Jane was able simultaneously to deliver the training, fix the technology problems, and once again create value for the clients.

Jane should have felt a sense of elation, having done a good job under difficult circumstances. Instead, she felt drained, angry, and used. Why? While Jane was conducting the training, a few people from the home office started sending her e-mails and phone messages telling her what she already knew: that the technology was not working and required immediate attention. Even after the training was completed successfully, the same critics continued with the critical e-mails and calls.

Jane sat at her desk and fumed. "Even if I were an employee receiving a salary for this work," she told herself, "this is no way to treat people!" Jane had about ten minutes before she had to talk to another client from a different law firm. She knew she had to pull herself together and get over this emotional experience; otherwise it would color every interaction for the rest of the day.

Put Yourself in Jane's Shoes

Jane has ten minutes to recover from this dissonant experience so that she can have the next conversation with new clients and not infect them with her dark and stormy emotions. If you were Jane, what would you do in the next ten minutes?

____

____

____

____

____

Resonance in Action: Your Turn

Recall an occasion when you were keenly aware that your emotional state of being was being corrupted by someone else's dissonance.

What do you remember feeling and thinking?

I remember feeling these emotions:

I remember thinking these thoughts:

What happened next? Were you able to pull yourself out of spiraling into dissonance or did you lose your balance and equanimity?

Either way, what were your interactions with others like immediately afterward?

How did *you feel* after those interactions?

Perhaps you can recall a time when the dissonance of another person or group influenced you. To some degree, emotional intelligence, particularly skills such as self-awareness and social awareness, can help to insulate us from a dissonant environment. In Jane's case, her self-awareness allowed her to distinguish her personal sense of worth from the criticism she was hearing, and her social awareness allowed her to focus on service to the client rather than on unhelpful comments from others. Nevertheless, dissonance is distracting and destructive. Jane was shaken by the experience, and her future encounters with that client and others were affected by this bad experience. Rather than walking into the office with optimism and joy, she felt like the old comic strip character Joe Btfsplk, the man in the L'il Abner cartoon who walked around with a small, dark cloud hovering above his head and brought bad luck to everyone he encountered. Worse yet, Jane felt anxiety and despair about the work she found herself doing for this company. She knew she should be grateful, but the benefits of the work simply did not exceed the terrible way she felt almost every time she had to interact with this particular client. For Jane's Renewal Coach to be helpful, their conversations had to address two important issues. The first was to develop actions that would empower Jane to address personal and organizational dissonance. Second, they had to consider how she could seek other opportunities for meaningful work with this client and with others so that she could sustain the energy she needed to be effective.

IF RESONANCE IS A STRENGTH

If your resonance score was in the 41 to 70 range, you are one of those people who are really terrific to be around. This is not only because you are emotionally aware of yourself and others, but also because you use compassion, which means you have a knack for understanding what others feel while also helping them take action to improve their situation. As a coach, you exude balance and presence. You neither empathize to the point of collusion with other people's strong emotions nor do you assume that you have all the answers.

Resonance, however, must be nurtured and maintained. Boyatzis and McKee (2005) remind us that leadership is demanding and that often, simply because of its nature, it creates distance between people and as a result can feel very, very, lonely. They tell us that leaders who neglect their own personal renewal fall prey to what they call the "syndrome of sacrifice, stress, and dissonance" (p. 7). To take care of your resonance it is important to be mindful of your connection to others and of how much you mean to the people in your personal and professional lives. Being mindful that your words, demeanor, and emotions make a difference for others makes you humble and tender. When you understand how much you mean to others, you realize you have power to inspire and transmit courage, and you choose every day and in every interaction to connect to your own purpose on the planet.

Do You Know How Much You Matter to Others?

What is your first reaction when someone tells you that you have made a difference for him or her?

Do you know how much you matter to people? If you did, what is it about you that they are responding to?

People who know how much they matter to others treat every conversation with them as if it matters. What do you do to treat every conversation with others as if it matters?

Whom do you love to be around? What is it about them that makes them matter so much to you?

What are the characteristics of the people you love to be around that you wish to learn, practice, and emulate?

IF RESONANCE IS A WEAKNESS

If you scored either in the 10 to 40 range or the 71 to 100 range on the Resonance Assessment and are fed up with yourself and your own pessimistic emotions, be of good cheer! This means you are aware of the fact that you are depleted of the elements that stimulate resonance, mindfulness, hope, and compassion (Boyatzis & McKee, 2005), and that it is time for you to take steps to engage in personal and professional renewal.

When it comes right down to it, resonance has an awful lot to do with happiness. Unhappiness about any aspect of your life is like a pebble in your shoe in the twentieth mile of a marathon. You simply cannot go on until you remove it. Happiness is all about your life, including the work you have chosen to do, the quality of your relationships, where you are living, your health, your goals, your sense of efficacy, your spirituality, your love life, the realization of your dreams, and ultimately your own personal judgment about the quality of your life, your purpose on the planet, and whether or not you are living your purpose. We know, this sounds like a large number of plates to keep spinning at the same time. The truth is that these indicators of happiness are rarely perfect at any given time. Strangely, we would not want them to be. If they were always perfect, we would not have enough dissatisfaction to get us to change, or to learn something new, or to broaden our perspective, or to replace an old habit with something better. The following activity asks you to specify what makes you happy and what you feel when you do not do these things. After you have completed the activity, ask yourself if overall your behavioral and emotional patterns add to or subtract from your resonance.

Behavioral and Emotional Patterns

To become more resonant, begin by recognizing the behavioral and emotional patterns in your life that

- Elicit optimism and helpful emotions each day and over the long term for yourself and others.
- Involve and support others.
- Transmit positive emotions and contribute to the greater good.

Consider the following four areas and write as many responses as come to mind:

These are the things that make **me** personally happy day to day (for example, running four miles, meeting the gang for Friday happy hour, meditating every morning, going on a date with my spouse or partner every Saturday, playing the organ, eating six fruits and vegetables each day, taking the dog to the park, cooking one new recipe each week, writing six pages of my novel per day):

____

____

____

____

____

____

____

____

This is what I feel when I don't do these things:

____

____

____

____

____

(continued)

Behavioral and Emotional Patterns (continued)

These are the things that support ***others*** day to day and that make me happy when I do them (for example, collaborating with my team, analyzing indicators toward our goals, developing new processes, learning together, picking up my daughter from after-school care exactly at 5:15 P.M. and going directly to the park to play before dinner, breaking through dilemmas with coworkers or family members):

____

____

____

____

____

This is what I feel when I don't do these things:

____

____

____

____

____

These are the things I do that are building blocks and requirements for the vision I have of the life I want (for example, getting that new degree or certification, working with a coach to finish writing my book, taking a leadership role in a professional organization, learning how to use the video camera and posting clips on YouTube, volunteering with a mentor to learn skills I will need in order to do meaningful work):

____

____

____

____

____

This is what I feel when I don't do these things:

____

____

Behavioral and Emotional Patterns (continued)

These are the things I do that benefit myself and others over the long haul, to achieve a greater good (for example, establishing a group of people committed to doing something for a cause, donating a percentage of profits from my business to a cause I care about, volunteering my time and talents to promote others in need, setting up programs and policies that encourage my coworkers or family members to do what matters to them, refining processes in order to care for the environment, telling and showing clients how much they mean to me):

This is what I feel when I don't do these things:

Waking Up to Resonance

What you feel when you do not do the things that make you happy are the alarms to which you need to pay attention. They reveal the source of your dissonance. When you notice them, take immediate action to replenish your sources of happiness.

Adele, a successful nurse with a doctoral degree, is in her fifties and working in a prestigious university hospital. She is now reflecting on her late teens and early twenties, recalling her headstrong nature and a consistent tendency to do exactly the opposite of whatever an authority figure told her to do. Adele recalls being completely aware that she was making choices that were not always in her best interest, demonstrating a terrific capacity for self-awareness, one of the competencies of emotional intelligence. Back then, however, she did not know how to pull herself out of the strong emotions of anger, resentment, and powerlessness, and more often than not she got herself involved in painful situations. She recalls thinking, "What am I doing? What am I doing? I am messing up what could be my life." This repeated sequence in Adele's youthful years created a strong emotional memory for her that serves her well today. When she feels those same emotions coming over her, she knows what they mean and she now has the ability and wisdom to interrupt her habitual response and mindfully choose to respond more resonantly.

Leaders who coach and coaches of leaders must take immediate action at the first signs that they are the source of dissonance, because while they are in a dissonant state of being, they have the potential of ruining the day for a lot of people—their clients and colleagues—who will go on and ruin the day for all the people they interact with, and so on and so forth. Here is an affirmation we use in our coaching practice to remind us to set aside our own crap when we are interacting with others and to attend to personal happiness so we can bring our best selves to our clients: "I am prepared to coach my clients with compassion, presence, and hope in order to support them in achieving their most cherished goals, to serve a greater good in their work, families, communities, and beyond."

NEXT STEPS IN THE 100-DAY RENEWAL PROJECT

Identify specific action steps that are inspired by your reflections in this chapter. Table 12.1 provides some sample steps in a 100-Day Renewal Project that bear directly on resonance.

Table 12.1 Samples of Actions That Will Activate Resonance Within This Project

Action Steps	People and Networks Engaged
Keep a daily journal of ten bulleted sentences naming what made me feel happy. At the end of each week, notice categories, patterns, and frequencies.	A trusted colleague, friend, or mentor
Gauge the level of optimism about this project by asking those involved to anonymously rate themselves from 1 to 10 on an index card on how optimistic they feel about this project's success. Collect the cards, tally the numbers, chart, and discuss the results.	Immediate team; extend to others affected by the project as time goes on
Meet with other manager-leaders in the organization to share the anticipated systemic impact of this project. Ask for feedback about what impact it will have on them.	Systemwide manager-leaders
Schedule a walk-and-talk brainstorm session for our group with the goal that each group of three will have ten possible solutions to a current dilemma.	Immediate team
Review the vision statements of internal and external clients and note what they have in common with this project. Hold a follow-up focus group to obtain additional information about what could be leveraged in this project to support their vision.	Work teams, managers, leaders

Brainstorm your own actions in the following table. You may also return to the 100-Day Renewal Project template we introduced in Chapter Six and enter your actions there. Be sure to use the LEAD technique:

What do you need to LEARN?
What EVIDENCE do you need to collect and analyze?
What ATTITUDES and expectations must be developed?
What DECISIONS must be made?

Action Steps	People and Networks Engaged

COACHING CONVERSATION

Let's return to Jane, whom we met at the opening of this chapter.

"I almost lost it yesterday," Jane told her coach as she recounted the story about the Internet presentation's technological glitch.

"What a challenging situation," her coach agreed. "I'm particularly struck by the realization you had that the home office people appeared not to have read the agenda but were telling you what to do. What did you think and feel at that moment?"

"Funny you ask about that," replied Jane. "Because out of all of this, that is what made me the most furious and dejected. I just can't imagine dealing with this client for much longer. The problem is they allow me to reach so many of the other legal firms that really do share the vision I have of greater protection for victims of domestic violence."

"This is a dilemma, indeed," said her coach. "But you just put your finger on something important. That is, that this company gives you access to many of the smaller firms that need and want your help."

"Exactly true," said Jane. "But I need either to protect myself better from their negativity or to do something to turn it around."

"Tell me," said the coach, "What did you do in the ten minutes you had between the end of that presentation and the next call you had with a different client? How did that call turn out?"

"It may sound funny but I resisted the first impulse I had, which was to reply sharply and defensively to the e-mail they sent; but knowing I had another call in ten minutes stopped me from doing that. I knew I could never compose the e-mail I wanted to in that short time! That turned out to be my saving grace, because what I did instead was breathe in and out, very slowly, the way I learned in my yoga class. With each breath I felt less like hammering out an angry response. In fact, here it is one day later and I still have not responded, although I know I need to."

Let's pause for a moment. Before you read any further, consider your own reaction to what Jane has said.

What other questions could you ask?

___

___

___

___

___

Are there other patterns that Jane might recognize? If so, what questions would you raise to help her consider those patterns?

___

___

___

___

___

Jane appears to have come to a significant conclusion. What could go wrong? How can you help her minimize the impact of a decision that is dissonant?

___

___

___

___

___

"Sounds like the breathing gave you some time and space between those initial emotions and the action they typically instigate, and now you feel ready to respond more positively. I wonder: because this client is important, you have a chance to respond just to this situation, but this might also be an opportunity to influence this company on a larger scale. What do you think about that?"

"Oh, this is definitely an opportunity to change some old patterns," said Jane. "For example, I've observed over and over that this company engages in a common pattern of lengthy back-and-forth communication explaining why things went wrong, developing processes to make sure it never happens again, and generally leaving some people glad they were not the ones who screwed up this time. Frankly, I don't have time for that."

"What would be a different way of responding to the critical e-mail they sent to you right after receiving it? How do you feel like responding?"

"What I really want to do is write a five-word response, 'Thank you for your feedback!' That would blow their minds!"

"What stops you from writing that response?"

"Well, I know it sounds kind of flippant; I suppose that is what stops me. If I really want to use this situation as an opportunity to create more optimism in my future dealings with this company, and if I want to stay on track with helping the other law firms to which they give me access, to make a difference in domestic violence cases, I guess I'd like to put more into my reply."

"Is what you don't say, then, just as important or perhaps even more important than what you do say?" asked the coach. "For example, you mentioned this might be an opportunity to break the back-and-forth cycle of explanation, defensiveness, and time wasted developing policy to ensure that this doesn't happen again. So what do you think you would let go of in your message back to them?"

"Excellent question," said Jane. "This really excites me because if I just don't even go there at all—you know, all the explaining and rationalization and defensiveness—but simply thank them for the feedback and then add a few sentences about how the panel allowed these law firms to share strategies for making a difference in domestic abuse cases, I could change the whole feel of the incident. Even if they don't change their practices, it sure feels better to me!"

Resonance and Renewal

By responding differently than expected, Jane changed the typical trajectory of the entire exchange. Her response triggered a different response in her home office colleagues, and that allowed Jane to see a surprising side to them. Instead of this exchange becoming a withdrawal of goodwill in relationships on both sides, it became a chance to build and nurture them. Better yet, Jane began to think about how dissonance can be interrupted at any time when she remembers the greater good that gives meaning to her life and work.

In the next chapter we examine the next part of the Renewal Coaching framework: relationship.

CHAPTER 13

Relationship
When Process Is Personal

Passion, intimacy, and commitment are the hallmarks of great relationships. Coaching relationships are no exception. The important work of Renewal Coaching, which is the realization of a greater good, requires that both coach and client feel excitement, energy, and desire for the work (passion); a willingness to engage in conversations that reveal the truth about who the coach and client are in their respective roles (intimacy); and demonstrable action to go the distance in both good times and tough times (commitment).

At any given time during Renewal Coaching, at least two person-to-person relationships are in play: first, the relationship between coach and client (or coaching leaders and employees); second, the relationships the clients have with the people and networks through which they work to accomplish their goals. An additional relationship is the one between clients and the work itself, including the greater good they seek to influence. In fact, many people speak about their work as if it were a relationship. They say, "I love my work" or "I hate my work," or even, "I'm staying in this job just until I get the kids through college, then I'm out of here!"

Just as in any healthy relationship, Renewal Coaches do not have control over the choices made by the people they coach but in every interaction must rely instead on compassionate tools, such as listening, questioning, and calling for commitments to action and accountability. These tools strengthen relationships.

Relationship Assessment Review

Take a moment to review your Relationship Assessment from Chapter Four. If you have not yet taken the assessment, please do so by logging on to www.RenewalCoaching.com and selecting Assessments.

My Relationship Assessment score: ____________________

Key insights from my responses to the open-ended questions in the Resonance Assessment:

____

____

____

____

____

RELATIONSHIP MOMENTS

Davis is manager of a medium-sized city branch of a well-known financial services institute that embraces several socially aligned business initiatives that allow it simultaneously to drive social change and strengthen business objectives and strategies. In the past three years, companywide indicators of these strategies in action and the results they achieve have maintained or gone up slightly. Yet when Davis disaggregated the data to compare his branch to other branches around the country, he was dismayed by what he saw. Indicators revealed dismal performance for community volunteer hours, contributions to foundations, engaged employees, and contributions to the employee grant program, which is a source of funds to employees who experience natural disaster or personal crisis.

When he raised the topic with his management team they shook their heads and reminded him that the whole country was in recession and this was just another symptom of a larger system failure. For the first time Davis noticed that his team was speaking from a sense of disempowerment and fear. They truly believed there was nothing they could do until the national economy improved. Wherever Davis went in the community, entrepreneurs and small business owners told him how discouraged they felt about the national economy and the various government-funded bailouts for large companies that had begun in 2008. Where was help for the "little guy"? they asked.

Davis had been thinking that his region could offer pro-bono financial consulting, much like lawyers do for their services, directly to the entrepreneurs and small business owners in their community. Pro-bono financial consulting would demonstrate real concern for the "little guy" who was struggling to find a way to keep afloat. Davis realized that this was a departure from the current model in which employees could volunteer up to four hours per month to any cause in which they personally believed. The pro-bono work would be very focused on providing financial consulting to those who needed it and was one new initiative that Davis wanted to discuss with his team. But secretly he harbored an even more radical idea, one that he was hesitant to bring up to his team, given their pessimism.

Davis had been thinking for a while about the company commitment to "wealth management" for people who were financially well off. This was an important service for the majority of their clients, but he could not help but notice the unquestioned and much less optimistic language—such as "debt management" and "financial literacy for low-income consumers"—that was used in the financial community at large to refer to those who are not well off. Davis wanted to propose to his team that they think out of the box and partner with various grassroots community groups to provide pro-bono financial services to women and minority-owned businesses and create hopeful and optimistic programs—with the language to match—for the vast majority of people in the community, who in the long run did not want to settle for managing their debt but wanted to create and manage assets.

Davis knew his management team was not exempt from the discouraging state of the economy, including the predictions of continued gloom and doom for at least the next two years. This was on top of the fact that their branch already lagged behind in the existing social initiative indicators. But he also knew the economy would eventually improve and he believed his company could lead the way for more people to feel financially empowered in the future.

Davis's Story

What do you infer about Davis and his vision for the people in his community? Think about areas of leverage, challenges, and political capital.

____

____

____

____

____

In general, what are all the relationships and networks connected to Davis's vision, both inside and outside the company?

____

____

____

What topics and issues will Davis need to have knowledge about before he brings up his ideas to his management team?

____

____

____

Take a few minutes now to complete the following worksheet in order to explore the nature of relationship within your 100-Day Renewal Project.

Relationship in Action: How Do You Get People to Care?

What is your 100-Day Renewal Project going to change about the current reality?

Who will be touched by those changes and in what way?

Why do you want to make a difference in these relationships? What will it lead to?

There are times when other people do not care about what matters to you and some people will choose what they perceive as self-preservation over the greater good. Can you let that go?

(continued)

Relationship in Action: How Do You Get People to Care? (continued)

Which relationships are so strong already that you can call upon them now to move this project forward? What will you ask them to do?

Which relationships will you have to nurture? Why is this so?

How do you currently show people that you care? What do you do on a daily basis to support the people who are closest to you in your work and life?

IF RELATIONSHIP IS A STRENGTH

If you scored between 71-100 points on this assessment, not only do you have strong ties with other people in your life, but as a result, you also have more political capital to work with which will cause others to rally around your project and proposals and initiate ideas about how they can help.

Although you are more likely to find others who are interested in your project, there are still several relationship values that imply actions you can take to ensure support and engagement from various people and networks including your coach (if you have one) or the person (people) you coach, other coworkers, and the greater context of the organization. The following worksheet challenges you to deepen your self-awareness and your understanding of relationship.

Relationships

For each relationship value, respond to the questions that follow.

Vulnerability

Coaches want clients to express their greatest hopes and fears. They create a safe place for the client to do this by listening, withholding judgment, maintaining confidentiality, and acknowledging the importance of the client's perspective.

How often do you express your greatest hopes and fears and encourage others to do the same? What stops you from doing this?

What is your reputation for confidentiality?

Authenticity

Clients articulate exactly what they want to see happen and why it is important to them. When you tell people what it means to you instead of trying to coerce them into believing, this is good for them; they are more likely to become involved.

Think of a project you started or wanted to start that meant a lot to you. Who did you involve and what do you remember about how you first presented the idea? Is your tendency to tell people how they will benefit from your ideas or to tell people what the project means to you?

(continued)

Relationships (continued)

Self-Intimacy

Coaches encourage clients to reflect deeply about who they are *becoming* as a result of following through on a project. This is an opportunity for clients to clarify their purpose on this planet and the meaning of their life and work.

In Chapter Four you identified a greater good to which you want to contribute and that would give meaning to your life. Assuming that your passion for this purpose is fueled in some part by what you have learned from responding proactively to challenges in your life, what do you think is the relationship between adversity and resilience?

____

____

____

____

____

____

____

____

Commitment

Ensure that the people who align their energy with your project have what they need to be successful. Follow through on your commitment to help them maintain their focus. Eliminate or repurpose existing demands that draw energy away from the shared vision.

In the following table, write down specific instances of working with people, teams, and networks on a previous important project. Then record exactly what you did to ensure their success.

People	Resources to Ensure Their Success

Honesty

Coaches, clients, and coworkers are willing to voice theories; ask tough, provocative questions; and probe for deeper understanding of the issues to illuminate root causes.

Relationships (continued)

What hard truths have you shared with people who are important to you?

____

____

____

____

____

What hard truths have people who are important to you told you in your lifetime? What impact did those words have on you?

____

____

____

____

____

Summary

Review your responses to the preceding prompts. Mark with a highlighter pen the words and sentences that you determine to be important in the particular project you are now undertaking.

IF RELATIONSHIP IS A WEAKNESS

For most people, close relationships are a source of happiness and comfort. They provide safe harbor from life's troubles. Loving relationships even ward off loneliness, which is connected to several health problems, including cardiovascular disease (Lynch, 2000). If "relationship" as an element in the Renewal Coaching model is a weakness for you, take heart. Whether you have mistakenly decided that self-reliance means you don't need other people, or if you are fed up with being burned in personal relationships and have chosen to be neglectful of relationships with others yourself, there are steps you can take to make fast improvements.

Decide to Let Go

What is your history with important relationships? If you scored in the 10 to 40 range, you may be so self-reliant that no one else can really get close to you. If this sounds like you, list the names of the people (work, romantic, family, friends) who taught you it was better to be alone and do things yourself than to join with others in a common vision:

If you scored in the 41 to 70 range, you may have suffered the loss of so many relationships to which you gave your all but received nothing in return that you are now jaded. List the names of the people in your past relationships (work, romantic, family, friends) who taught you it is too risky to be in relationships:

Now, for each person on your list, identify at least one lesson that person taught you that you could say is a gift or a benefit of the relationship. Maybe it was joy doing one certain thing, or maybe it was a skill they had that you admired:

What Did You Give?

The point to the preceding exercise was to make you aware that most relationships are neither all good nor all bad, even when you or the other person chooses to end them. For each of the relationships you just listed, what are the gifts you gave to the other person?

___

___

___

Given what you were able to receive and give in the relationships you wrote about, what relationship talents do you have that you could now apply to achieve what matters to you?

___

___

___

Describe what will happen when your relationships with people who are important to you are going well. What are you doing? What will help when you feel yourself slipping back into your default mode of going it alone?

___

___

___

TAKING CARE OF OTHERS

Relationships are of course two-way streets. Imagine how grateful you will feel when your project is a success because other people were willing to support you and align their energies with yours. What supports will these people need from you in return? In your work, volunteer, or community life, for example, people may need support in the form of time, resources, tools, and policies. In your personal life, people may need your time, attention, and love.

How Will You Get Behind the People Who Get Behind You?

Name the people, team, network, or group you need to support:

____

____

____

____

____

In each case, list the specific support they need from you as they support you in your goals:

____

____

____

____

____

NEXT STEPS IN THE 100-DAY RENEWAL PROJECT

Identify specific action steps inspired by your reflections in this chapter. Table 13.1 provides some sample steps in a 100-Day Renewal Project that bear directly on relationship.

Brainstorm your own action steps in the following table. You may also return to the 100-Day Renewal Project template introduced in Chapter Six and enter your actions there. Be sure to use the LEAD technique:

What do you need to LEARN?
What EVIDENCE do you need to collect and analyze?
What ATTITUDES and expectations must be developed?
What DECISIONS must be made?

Table 13.1 Samples of Actions That Will Activate Relationships (Using Davis's Story as an Example)

Action Steps	People and Networks Engaged
Disaggregate all data about the volunteer activities of employees in the community.	Business results group, HR data
Research and list all community organizations and networks that reach nontypical clients of the organization. Contact them and ask about their needs.	Immediate team, community groups
Write out my own thoughts about why I am drawn to this project. Meet with my core team and tell them what this project means to me.	Coach, close friend, core team
Calculate the cost and benefits of dedicated pro-bono hours. What important skills, knowledge, and experience will our employees gain through this plan?	Business and HR managers
Hold volunteer focus groups with employees who are intrigued with joining the pro-bono group and ask them to contribute ideas to make the program work.	All interested employees
Meet with leaders of the community nonprofit groups and ask them to contribute ideas to make the program work.	Community leaders and program coordinators
Audit the language used throughout the company: all marketing materials, collateral materials, signage, Web site, communication. Is it optimistic and representative of the desired vision of our clients?	Work with VP of marketing; have initial conversation with home office
Identify indicators of success and set up a database.	Division heads and technology business team
Pilot several pro-bono engagements and monitor the identified indicators.	Employee-led pilot groups
Communicate pilot results internally, to the board and to the stakeholder groups. Solicit feedback for improvement and commit to a second, more refined round.	Communications, HR, chairpeople
Devise the recognition program for participating employees.	Cross-divisional group of stakeholders

Action Steps	People and Networks Engaged

COACHING CONVERSATION

Davis told his coach, "Our regional indicators for socially aligned business objectives are all lower than those of other regions. Yet we live in one of the poorer states, where people are really hurting. I never noticed the disconnect between the volunteer work our employees do and the business we are in. I mean, we are finance consultants; couldn't we be helping people with their finances?"

"Let me see if I understand," said Davis's coach. "Although your employees volunteer time to organizations, your office lags behind those indicators compared to other offices. On top of that, you see an opportunity for them to volunteer in finance—the business you are in."

"Yes, that's right," said Davis. "We have small businesses failing left and right in the state. I've been thinking about a pro-bono model like lawyers use to volunteer their legal services. We could help these businesses with their financial business planning."

"Who else have you talked to about this idea, Davis?"

"Actually, I haven't yet. Everyone is in a 'circle the wagon' mode. All they talk about is how bad business is. I'm afraid they wouldn't go for the idea of giving away their time for free."

"When you say 'everyone,' Davis, I wonder if that is entirely true. Have you had interactions with anyone on your team that would give you the idea they would be interested in hearing what you have to say?"

"Well, Marge, who is the HR director, is usually open to innovative ideas in personnel. But she has had to lay people off recently and I'm not sure she has the energy for this."

"Hmmm," the coach said. "Davis, you have a process in place with the senior team for brainstorming business ideas in response to ongoing environmental scans."

"You are right," said Davis. "I could put this on the agenda for next week's meeting and bring it up first to the whole team. Kind of raise the flag and see how they respond. Given the climate, however, I have to present persuasively the first time."

Davis

Let's pause for a moment. Before you read any further, consider your own reaction to what Davis has said so far.

What other questions could you ask?

____

____

____

What seem to be the significant relationship issues?

____

____

____

What additional information might Davis need before he presents his idea to the whole team?

____

____

____

"Davis, let me ask you this: Why does this idea mean so much to you?"

"Well, I happened to run into a friend who recently started a business. This is a guy who put his retirement into starting his business and now he might lose it all. I sat down with him and helped him restructure portions of his budget and it really opened some doors for him. It was easy for me to spend a few hours but it made a world of difference to him. That was when the lightbulb came on for me—that we could do this pro-bono."

"So this means a lot to you at a personal level—helping a friend and seeing the impact on him makes a compelling story. Is something stopping you from telling this story to your team?"

"I know times are hard for everyone right now, but today I noticed just how pessimistic my leadership team is. More than that, I realized that although we have some services for people who do not have a lot of wealth to manage, the language we use does not have a lot of hope in it. It is all about debt and low income. I see how that language is just an extension of where we spend our time."

"So you are seeing this as a more pervasive issue?"

"Yes, and interestingly enough, one that may cause us to miss an opportunity. The way I see it, a pro-bono financial consulting initiative is a triple win. First, we can help small business owners succeed—talking to my friend made that obvious. Second, when those small businesses succeed, they are likely to become loyal clients. Third, our consultants will get on-the-job training and experience through the consulting work they do."

"You've just articulated very well three ways this idea could make a difference. Is Marge, the HR director, the key person you need to involve?"

Davis replied, "Marge is crucial, of course. As is Pete, who leads the small business consulting division. Pete's department has been hit the hardest in terms of layoffs. Because of this, I anticipate he will have some objections. With a skeleton crew, he may not feel he can release people to pro-bono cases."

"Are there other responsibilities that could be redirected that would free up time?"

"That's a good question," said Davis. "Pete will have some ideas about that. I should also gather information about the number of small businesses in our region who might take advantage of this program if it was offered. Or maybe we can cap it from the start and pilot a few cases."

"You have some experience with that process from previous initiatives, as I recall," said the coach. "I suspect your friend would be willing to share some ideas about what made his experience with you so supportive."

"Yes, in fact, having a key group of small business owners involved from the beginning would make the project more sustainable even when the economy recovers. Bottom line, I feel we have an opportunity to lead a positive initiative that has benefits for all of the people involved."

Davis's conversation with his coach illustrates both the importance of relationships in Renewal Coaching and some approaches for acknowledging the personal side of renewal. Within complex systems, goal achievement requires the involvement and support of multiple people and networks within the system. This is even truer and more necessary when it comes to effecting a greater good, because the greater good, by its very nature, includes what is good for a larger number of people over a long period of time. Davis is a strong leader who sees both business and social opportunities within a serious economic challenge. He cares about the people he works with and the people in his community, which does not prevent him from also referring to data to track indicators that matter.

CHAPTER 14

Renewal

Energy, Meaning, and Freedom to Sustain the Journey

Renewal provides individuals and organizations with energy to accomplish important goals and engage in meaningful work that has a social impact. People who direct their lives toward creating the greater good say this is what living a meaningful life is all about. Where there is renewal there is potential for a meaningful life, and when life and work have meaning, renewal is inherent.

More and more people seek meaningful work and a meaningful life. They want to make a difference, leave a legacy, and enjoy the time they have on this earth. Consider these surprising statistics from a career study carried out by Encore, a movement for work that matters in the second part of life: 50 percent of Americans ages fifty to seventy want work that helps others; this statistic rises to 58 percent for Baby Boomers (ages fifty to fifty-nine) (Hannon, 2009).

It is not only men and women in their forties and beyond who want meaningful circumstances in which they can both do well for themselves and make a difference for others. Dubbed the Millennial Generation, people born between 1980 and 2000 are described as confident, optimistic, goal oriented, inclusive, and civic minded (Howe and Strauss, 2000). They were instructed by parents and teachers and through key events in their formative years (the bombing of the Murrah Federal Building in Oklahoma City, the Columbine school shootings, 9/11) to care about the greater good. These inspiring young people are making a difference in the workplace and in their communities, and because communication and social networking technologies are second nature to them, they are doing it faster and more efficiently than the Boomers ever thought possible. Check out Web sites such as www.causecast.com, a "one-stop philanthropy shop," for a great example of how these young social activists are collaborating at a global level to make the world a better place.

Personal renewal can be found in the root of high places—that is, at the source of human greatness. For many people this is about applying their greatest gifts, often gained through challenging opportunities, in the humblest of circumstances. Our research into what wise people do to live a meaningful life supports this theory as well. Here are just a few examples, and in every case we have used real names, with the authorization of these outstanding exemplars of renewal:

- Jonathan Sperling, a high school English teacher from Torrance, California, felt so discouraged about his students' lack of commitment to their learning that he started a movement called "I Care." Jonathan appealed directly to the students, telling them exactly how he felt as a teacher and what it would mean to him if they would begin to care about themselves and others. To his amazement, the students responded with ideas of their own about what they could do to inspire and encourage one another. Jonathan now says that because of "I Care," teaching "feels like a calling."
- Native American artist and activist Charlene Teters, as a young woman earning her master's degree from the University of Illinois, watched the sadness and confusion on the faces of her own two children at a football game where "Chief Illini," the team mascot, danced on the football field. Char began what is now an international movement to challenge and remove images of Native Americans from marketing materials and sports events. She says, "I had no choice. I realized there were children everywhere being damaged by this." (Charlene's work is the subject of a documentary by Jay Rosenstein; visit http://charleneteters.com.)
- Wallace Howard, previously a kindergarten teacher from North Carolina, told us, "I had a hard time learning to read as a kid, so I figured I'd better be a kindergarten teacher. Little did I know that kindergarten would

become the main place for kids to learn to read!" From his experience, Wallace developed his own program to help struggling readers. When he was told he had to stop using the program because it was not on the list of board-approved material, Wallace quit his teaching job in spite of being just a few years from retirement and now trains other teachers all over the country to use his methods (www.makinggreatreaders.com).

- Mark Cerney was on his honeymoon when his beloved childhood caretaker, MiMi, passed away in the nursing home that Mark had provided for her. Because he was not a blood relative, however, the nursing home never called him, and MiMi was buried without anyone in attendance. Stunned by the loss of MiMi, Mark learned that his experience was not uncommon. In response, he founded the Next of Kin Registry (NOKR), a secure and confidential online receptacle where people can go to enter information about themselves and about who emergency and medical personnel should contact in case they are sick or injured, or if they die (www.NOKR.org).

You can find more stories of renewal, redemption, and people working for the greater good at www.encore.org and www.wisdomout.com as well as at many other sites on the Internet and in books in the bookstores. Personal and organizational renewal is the key to sustainable change that will make a difference in the world today and in the future.

Renewal Assessment Review

Take a moment to review your Renewal Assessment from Chapter Four. If you have not yet taken the assessment, please do so by logging on to www.RenewalCoaching.com and selecting Assessment.

My Renewal Assessment score: ____________________

Key insights from my response to the open-ended questions in the Renewal Assessment:

____

____

____

____

____

RENEWAL MOMENTS

Jock Brandis was a talented lighting director in the film industry, not to mention something of a problem-solving tinkerer, a much needed commodity on demanding film sets where he was called on to solve unique mechanical problems. In 2002, after the death of his wife, a friend asked Jock to go to a village in Mali, Africa, to repair a water treatment system. While there, Jock met women who supported their families by shelling hard, dried peanuts for hours every single day. Jock assessed the situation and decided there had to be a better way and he promised to return in a year with some sort of mechanical solution.

Unable to find an existing machine to do the job he had promised, Jock decided to invent it himself. He first learned all he could about peanuts, even going to peanut expert President Jimmy Carter for advice. Then he designed what he calls the Universal Nut Sheller, a device that costs $28.00 in materials available in Mali and other countries and that can be easily reproduced. The sheller worked magnificently, and immediately contributed to improved economic, health, and social conditions in Mali.

In 2003 Jock and some Peace Corp friends formed the Full Belly Project, a nonprofit endeavor to invent low-tech solutions to puzzling mechanical problems, to form partnerships to create food-related economic opportunities, and to empower village food co-ops to operate successfully.

Even more remarkable are the practices and systems that Jock has created to sustain the work of the Full Belly Project:

- Jock doesn't just ship nut shellers, he ships the forms and blueprints so that villages can create as many of the shellers as they want to.
- Jock refuses to patent the universal nut sheller; he wants other people to replicate it and improve it.
- Designs for the sheller are on the Internet—free for anyone to download.
- Jock mentors interns from MIT and gives them free reign to collaborate and invent.
- Jock is directly involved in hands-on invention of the tools distributed by Full Belly.
- The Full Belly workshop is completely staffed by volunteers.

Learning from Jock

What do you infer about Jock because of his renewal journey? Think about Jock's attitudes, values, habits, and perspectives on his life:

Who else do you know who has some of the same personal qualities and perspectives you see in Jock? What do you notice about his or her life?

If you could have a one-on-one conversation with Jock, what would you ask him?

Is there anything about Jock's process that reminds you of your own life?

RENEWAL IN ACTION

Take a few minutes now to explore the patterns of renewal in your own life.

Renewal in My Life

What are the specific challenges inherent in the project you have identified?

How do you feel when you think about the challenges you just wrote about? Do you feel excitement or dread, or a little of both?

Explain why:

Who will you reach out to and count on as you move forward in your project? Why them?

Think of all the endeavors you have undertaken in which you were wildly successful and felt great about life. What did you do to keep up your momentum? How did you take care of yourself?

Who is inspired by you?

Renewal in My Life (continued)

Who is in your court, always ready to listen, ready to support, and even to jump in and get behind your dreams? How will you involve these people in your project?

What can't you wait to learn?

IF RENEWAL IS A STRENGTH

Jim Collins, author of the best-selling book *Good to Great: Why Some Companies Make the Leap . . . and Others Don't,* wrote, "It is impossible to have a great life unless it is a meaningful life. And it is very difficult to have a meaningful life without meaningful work" (2001, p. 210). If you scored between 71 and 100 on the Renewal Assessment, you not only have insight about what makes you feel happy and optimistic, but you also most likely describe your life as meaningful.

Renewal is a journey, not a place you finally arrive at and remain, never to be renewed again. The questions you need to ask yourself are these: Where am I holding myself back? Where am I stopping short?

Write your responses to the following questions:

Where am I stopping short in taking care of myself day to day? What could I do to follow through on making time to engage in hobbies, rest, relaxation, and physical, emotional, and spiritual activities?

____

____

____

____

____

Where am I stopping short in following through on developing the skills and knowledge needed for the life I envision? What experiences am I putting off?

____

____

____

Where am I stopping short in following through on taking action that develops other people?

____

____

____

Where am I stopping short in understanding what would make my life meaningful? How can I increase the work I am doing for the greater good?

____

____

____

What a Meaningful Life Creates for Others

Consider your responses to the previous questions as you complete the following table. In the first column, list all of the observations you made about Jock's qualities. In the second column, write your opinion about what those qualities allowed Jock to do. In the third column, record what these qualities led to for other people in Jock's life.

Jock's Qualities	What These Qualities Allowed Jock to Do for Others	What They Allowed Other People to Do in Their Own Lives

Now repeat the exercise for your own life.

Your Qualities	What These Qualities Allow You to Do for Others	What They Allow Others to Do in Their Own Lives

Finally, reflect on what you just wrote. How far are you willing to go to ensure that your life and work are everything you dream of?

____

____

____

____

____

IF RENEWAL IS A WEAKNESS

If your renewal score reveals some hard truths, please do not be discouraged. Hard truths combined with support are defining moments. They are forks in the road and you are in the driver's seat. If you have a Renewal Coach or you are using the Renewal Coaching framework to support someone else, this is an opportunity to make a difference.

If you scored in the range of 10 to 40, you need to take immediate steps to care for yourself before any other action. What have you been ignoring with reference to your physical, emotional, relationship, intellectual, and spiritual needs? Most of us have some idea of what ails us. This is an opportunity to take action on your own behalf.

For the following categories, write the first words that come to your mind when you think of what is missing in your life.

Physical needs:

Emotional needs:

Relationship needs:

Intellectual needs:

Spiritual needs:

Perhaps you have heard the expression, "You can't give a dollar if a quarter is all you have in your pocket." Sometimes we are depleted because we are trying to keep pace with the demands of other people around us who themselves are depleted and have imposed their approach to life on us or the person being coached.

Why are you depleted? Is the situation temporary or has this been going on for a long time?

Who cares about you and would support you in your renewal plan? Write their names here:

(continued)

What could you do to take immediate action? What will you do?

____

____

____

If you scored in the range of 41 to 70 on the Renewal Assessment, you may still be searching for the work or the calling, whether paid or volunteer, that makes your life meaningful. At this point it will be helpful for you to return to Chapter Three and take another pass at the exercises provided there. Because you are perceived to be successful—meeting goals, earning good money and accolades from others—you probably have a full agenda and calendar. In order to have time to pursue what makes your life meaningful, however, you will need to weed your garden. What you give your time and attention to will grow. This is true for relationships, learning, work, skills, and hobbies.

What will you take off your plate to make room for what matters most to you? Write your answers in the spaces provided.

This is what matters most to me right now:

____

____

____

To accomplish what matters most to me, I must stop doing the following:

____

____

____

What scares me about that and how will I manage it?

____

____

____

NEXT STEPS IN THE 100-DAY RENEWAL PROJECT

Identify specific action steps inspired by your reflections in this chapter. Table 14.1 provides some sample steps in a 100-Day Renewal Project that bear directly on renewal.

Now use the following table to brainstorm your own actions. You may also return to the 100-Day Renewal Project template introduced in Chapter Six and enter your actions there. Be sure to use the LEAD technique:

What do you need to LEARN?

What EVIDENCE do you need to collect and analyze?

What ATTITUDES and expectations must be developed?

What DECISIONS must be made?

Table 14.1 Samples of Actions That Will Activate Renewal

Action Steps	People and Networks Engaged
Identify and schedule personal renewal actions that sustain me day to day.	Coach, close friend, family member
Identify and schedule personal development actions that build my skills, knowledge, and experience and that extend over time and lead to increased capacity to contribute to a greater good.	Coach, learning groups, networks, places of expertise
Identify and schedule day-to-day renewal actions that contribute to the development of other people.	Coach, close friend, team, family
Identify and schedule long-term organizational (community or family) renewal projects that create meaningful life and work for myself and others and that have a social impact.	Coach, others affected, the larger environmental context
Communicate my commitment to my renewal actions and projects and be accountable for them and for reflecting on their impact on my life each day and over the long term and in the lives of others each day and over the long term.	Coach, others affected, the larger environmental context
Clarify for myself why this matters so much to me personally, and tell everyone I meet about what I am doing and why it matters.	Coach, family, friends, coworkers, extended social community
Broadly communicate through every means possible and to a global audience the process and outcomes of these renewal actions.	Global audience

(continued)

Table 14.1 *(continued)*

Action Steps	People and Networks Engaged
Seek out and participate, as a leader of ideas and action, with other people, networks, and organizations on a global scale who are also engaged in this work.	Global audience
Evaluate the impact of the actions associated with this project relative to all indicators: social, personal financial, emotional, physical, spiritual.	Coach, team, family, organization
Recognize accomplishments of myself and others and celebrate the impact of our work.	Coach, team, family, organization, global audience
Mentor other leaders who are passionate about this work.	Coach, team, family, organization, global audience
Advocate. Take action to affect state, national, and global policy and practice in order to bring this to scale.	Coach, team, family, organization, global audience

Action Steps	People and Networks Engaged

Action Steps	People and Networks Engaged

COACHING CONVERSATION

Roger is a senior communications specialist with a public relations firm that represents successful people in the arts, in science, in business, and in nonprofit organizations. The firm's clients are frequently seen in various print and visual media; their successes and contributions to their field are news.

"Roger, I'm very happy you have time to talk to me today in our scheduled coaching appointment. You cancelled our two previous sessions. What's been happening with you?"

"Where to begin?" Roger sighed. "Just between you and me, I am exhausted. I'm working day and night with our most demanding clients, who are spread out across the world in every time zone. So the calls, e-mails, faxes, teleconferences—they come every hour, every minute. Not only am I lacking sleep, but I am beginning to wonder why I even care."

"Sounds like you have been burning the candle at both ends, as they say, Roger," said the coach. "Now you have this hour with me to focus on yourself."

"Yes," Roger replied. "But I'm not even sure where to begin. You don't have control over my schedule, and I feel like I don't either."

"Let me ask you a few questions about that," said the coach. "Who do you feel is in control of your schedule?"

"Well, it is client driven, and because we tell them they can have access to us round the clock, 24/7, well, *all* my clients demand service round the clock. The most troublesome are those who imply we are not doing enough to put them and their accomplishments out in the media. They demand daily accounting of what we do to accomplish this for them. They don't understand that unless they have breaking news, not everyone is as interested in them as they think they should be."

"What role does your support staff have in the client response cycle?" asked the coach.

"I think they are feeling as burned out as I am. We have sort of a triage system in place, and they use it to assess each client contact to determine an appropriate response. This used to work, but it seems like we have a different breed of client these days. They are all so demanding."

"So the system previously worked, but now it does not seem to, and your sense is that it has to do with client expectations."

"Well, that's my first response," said Roger. "But I know enough to know that there is more to the story. I'm just not sure what all the variables are, and the bottom line is that even if I did, I'm not sure what can be done about it. It's like we've created our own monster."

"Roger, you've been successful at this work for many years, which is why the firm gives you the most visible clients. What else is different about your work now when you compare it to when you first got started in the business?"

"You know, when I was working my way up the ladder, proving to myself and others that I could handle anything on this job, I worked with the clients who were just getting started in their field. Most of them, I might add, were doing things that really mattered to them; there were the new authors with best-selling books, the researchers with breakthrough discoveries, the artists who came out of poverty. I used to enjoy the thrill of guiding them as they navigated their newfound success. I felt I had a hand in teaching them the ropes of celebrity with dignity."

"And now your entire client list is full of household names."

"Yes, that's right—and the money that comes with that is pretty nice, I have to admit. But I'm beginning to wonder if there isn't a better way.

I mean, there has to be, because I'll drop dead of a heart attack if I don't slow down. My wife is going to divorce me because I'm never home, and when I am I've got the cell phone glued to my ear. That's my real fear."

"That gets right to the heart of things," said the coach, "if you'll pardon the pun." The coach continued, "Roger, you've said some important things here that are clues to moving you forward. First, the heart-attack statement tells me you want to take some immediate control of your physical well-being. Second, in your reminiscence of the past when you 'raised' new clients to be empowered in their newfound success, your voice actually changed. You sounded calmer and, well, happier. Did I read that right?"

"You sure did," said Roger. "I've been thinking lately about my success. I no longer have to prove myself, so I'd like to do more of what I did when I got started. I may be an old guy, but I've got the experience to support these new, younger clients. Heck, I may even learn a thing or two in the process."

"Okay, so we are agreed that the two issues on the table for your own renewal are these: First, you want to take action to take better care of your physical needs—sleep, exercise, nutritious food, and relationships. Second, we'll look at strategies for you to rebalance your client caseload—add a few new clients who are at the start of their career."

As Roger and his coach continued their conversation over the next several months, Roger began to take specific action to transform his work situation and his life. He first clarified his personal vision and articulated to himself and others why this mattered to him. He had many conversations—with his boss, wife, clients, and colleagues. Some of them were difficult and others were surprisingly supportive. His schedule altered, as did a few habits. Roger learned about new people, new industries, even new technologies and psychologies.

What we hope you see in Roger's story is that he was at a crossroads. This was a defining moment for Roger. With his renewal coach, he saw the opportunity to transform his personal crisis, his disorienting dilemma, into growth. With his coach's help, Roger did not have to go it alone. He felt empowered to face and handle everything that came up with newfound energy, even as he was drawn forward by the meaning he derived from this important work.

PART FOUR

Sustaining

CHAPTER 15

Renewal Coaching in Action

As a result of your work in the previous chapters, you have reflected deeply on the results of the seven Renewal Coaching assessments and have achieved important insights about who you are and what makes your life and work meaningful. You have also created a 100-Day Renewal Project plan that pulls together the critical elements of Renewal Coaching and gives you an important tool for moving forward toward renewal, sustained change, and contribution to the greater good.

Now it is time to execute your 100-Day Renewal Project plan. Although some people can self-coach their way to renewal, most people need support from someone who understands their commitment to the greater good, the process of sustainable change, and the need for accountability and feedback. Whether you want to apply the Renewal Coaching perspective to your own life, are a leader who wants to use Renewal Coaching with the people with whom you work, or are already a working coach or new coach who wants to transform your practice to include the Renewal Coaching model, you don't have to go it alone. Consider the following options:

- If you do not have a coach and are now ready to embrace the Renewal Coaching perspective in your own work and life, you can visit www.RenewalCoaching.com and access our network of licensed renewal coaches.

- If you are a leader who wants to use Renewal Coaching as a development process with the people with whom you work, you have several options.
  - You can use the tools in this book and on the Renewal Coaching Web site to guide your interactions and introduce others to the processes.
  - You can engage a licensed renewal coach to work with you and your team to guide you through the processes and support you in implementation.
  - You can attend a Renewal Coaching institute and benefit from the support of the Renewal Coaching network as you work with your team and within your organization.
- If you are a working coach or about to begin your coaching career, you can become a licensed renewal coach and join the Renewal Coaching network and global community.

No matter which of these scenarios best describes your situation, there are people who want to support you. In our work with leaders in many organizations, we have found that those who have enjoyed the greatest success have two practices in common. First, they have written and executed 100-Day Renewal Project plans. They have taken time to translate the Renewal Coaching framework into detailed, specific, and immediate actions that have provided momentum for their journey. Second, they have reached out to other people in their lives for support and accountability. The exercises that follow will allow you to think through how you will move forward with support.

Who Cares About Your Renewal?

You mean a lot to the people who know and love you. Who cares that you have energy to live a meaningful life? Consider the areas of your life and list the names of people in them who care about you.

People who care about my physical health and well-being:

____

____

People who care about my emotional health and well-being:

____

____

People who care about my spiritual health and well-being:

____

____

People who care about the quality of my relationships:

____

____

People who care about my financial well-being:

____

____

People who care about my ______________ well-being:

____

____

Who Will Participate in Your Renewal Project?

Not only will it make a difference for you if you tell people in your life about your renewal project, but some of these people will be important contributors to your project. Reflect again on the names you have written down. Now, list those people you want to ask to play a role in the implementation of your plan.

People I want to involve in my plan implementation or who need to be involved:

____

____

What will you ask for?

Take one more pass at your list. What will you ask each person to do? Here are some things to consider:

Coach me.

Participate in the actions I take in a specific area.

Be an accountability partner for me by allowing me to report my progress on a regular schedule.

Be a cheerleader for me—give me positive feedback when you see me taking action.

Be an advocate for me—funnel resources, ideas, and people in my direction.

Develop your own renewal plan to complement mine. (team members at work, family members, friends who share your passion)

Mentor me. (people who have walked this path before me and can give me guidance)

Teach me a specific skill or process that I need in order to be successful.

Other?

People Who Will Help Me	My Specific Requests

Parting Words About Renewal Coaching in Action

The greater good, by definition, involves other people. Pursuit of the greater good is a social activity and you are not alone in your intent to give your life meaning through work that makes a difference. As you move forward, stay open to inspiration and support from surprising places. Be ready to cross industries, fields of thought, organizational structures, generations, societal structures, and political norms. Seed your mind with the understanding that people are remarkably connected, and that those connections are made visible when we find the courage to tell others what matters to us. The following activity asks you to brainstorm anyone and everyone who could be interested in your project.

Who Else Cares About This?

Remember the story from Chapter Fourteen about Jock Brandis, who called Jimmy Carter because he figured this president would know a thing or two about how to shell peanuts? You may not yet know their names and you may not yet know them personally, but you probably have some thoughts about the people, organizations, associations, and networks that will connect to and be involved in the meaningful work you are about to do. Brainstorm everything that comes to mind, no matter how unusual or improbable it sounds to you:

____

____

____

____

____

When and how will you follow up?

____

____

____

BACK TO YOUR 100-DAY RENEWAL PROJECT

Return to your 100-Day Renewal Project and revise your plan on the basis of the insights you received from the exercises in this chapter. What specific actions will you take in the next hundred days to involve other people in your project? Once again, use the LEAD technique:

What do you need to LEARN?
What EVIDENCE do you need to collect and analyze?
What ATTITUDES and expectations must be developed?
What DECISIONS must be made?

CHAPTER 16

Execution
Transforming Plans into Action

People and organizations in general do too much planning and not enough execution. The difference between what we know and what we actually do, famously described as the "knowing-doing gap" (Pfeffer & Sutton, 2000), has consequences that are far greater than the annual sigh that accompanies unfinished New Year's resolutions. Kotter (2006) concludes that the results of failed change efforts have "been appalling, with wasted resources and burned-out, scared, or frustrated employees" (p. 4). Worse yet, when plans overwhelm execution ability, it creates a mathematical certainty that even vital new initiatives will languish unfinished. The Law of Initiative Fatigue (Reeves, 2006b) states, "When resources of time, money, and emotional energy are held constant while the number of old, continuing, and new initiatives rises, organizational implosion is inevitable" (p. 107). This law is portrayed graphically in Figure 16.1. The horizontal axis represents the number of previous, current, and new initiatives. The vertical axis represents the resources available—money, time, emotional energy. As the number of initiatives increases (as shown by the upward progress of the curved line within the figure), the sheer enthusiasm and adrenalin—and perhaps the fear and terror—of new ideas can sustain you for a brief period. But after a while, as more and more initiatives are added to older ones but you have the same number of hours in the day and the same or declining resources in terms of money, people,

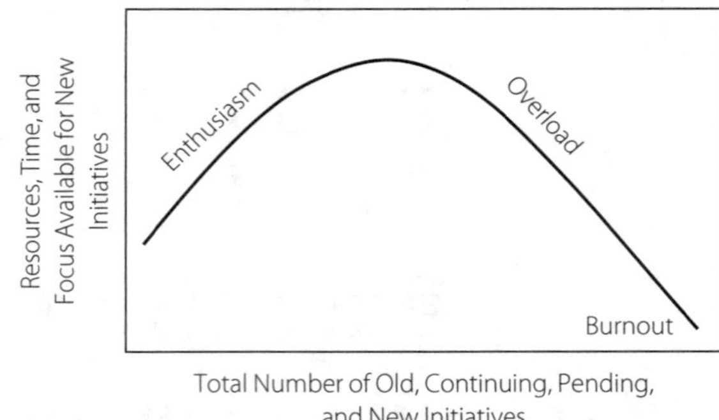

Figure 16.1 Focus: The Law of Initiative Fatigue

technology, and other assets, it is almost certain that your emotional and physical energy will flag. As the steeply declining line on the right side of the figure makes clear, it is impossible to execute your plan effectively if it is simply one more thing in your life.

DAILY DISCIPLINES FOR RENEWAL

In the next hundred days you will begin a pattern of activities and interactions that not only will determine the successful implementation of your plan but also will profoundly influence every area of your life. Renewal is not an event but a daily discipline. The literature of addiction and recovery offers many conflicting views of treatment, but one nearly unanimous conclusion is that people who are successful in their quest to stop addictive behavior do not merely experience a moment when they have recovered, as if a gangrenous limb had been amputated. People who have been sober for twenty years will speak candidly of the fact that they make a daily decision not to use drugs or alcohol. Executives who appear to have mastered organizational skills will nevertheless give themselves a couple of hours every month to stop, evaluate the degree to which they have returned to previous bad habits, and clear up their messes before they become catastrophic (Allen, 2001). People in thirty-year relationships who are totally committed and head over heels in love with one another will nevertheless schedule dates with the same seriousness with which they would schedule any business or volunteer commitment, because they know that without a regular structure, the weekly date can evaporate into a sea of conflicting commitments. Daily discipline is therefore required in order to succeed at this or at anything that is important for you, your family, or your organization.

CONFRONTING THE MYTHS THAT DEFEAT EXECUTION

The Multitasking Myth

In his splendid little book *The Myth of Multitasking: How "Doing It All" Gets Nothing Done*, Dave Crenshaw (2008) thoughtfully distinguishes between multitasking, the illusion of doing several things at the same time, and switch-tasking, the reality that takes place when people are attempting simultaneously to drive a car, send a text message, and have a conversation with their kids in the backseat. In fact, Crenshaw notes, this person is not doing three things at once, but rather is frantically and ineffectively switching among three different tasks. Such a driver is as dangerous as if she had been drinking, the text message is fragmentary and incoherent, and the kids are not fooled by the pretense of conversation. They know that again they are the least important part of this adult's life. The most pervasive multitasking that occurs today is when people answer e-mail and voice mail all day long, stopping whatever they are doing to respond to the beeping of their computer as surely as the dogs salivated in response to Dr. Pavlov's bell.

The Time-Management Myth

Aside from the "leap second" added to clocks once every century or so for the purposes of astronomical precision, the length of our day is rigidly consistent, and all of us have the same twenty-four hours in which to sleep, love, learn, and work. We can no more "manage time" than we can manage the sun. The only thing we can manage is ourselves—our daily decisions about what we will do with the time we have. The frequent complaint that "I don't have the time" is factually untrue. We all have precisely the same amount of time. What we lack is not time but rather a clear sense of priorities about how we will and will not spend time. Time management depends not on software programs, leather binders, or any external accoutrements. These only contribute to the illusion that we are managing time. The distinction between effective and ineffective execution is not the physical characteristics of the tools we use but the mental and emotional characteristics of the decisions we make.

The Strategic Planning Myth

You may be surprised at what profound results can be achieved from using such a simple tool as the 100-Day Renewal Project plan. After all, effective plans must be large, complex, and sophisticated. Personal planners must either reek of leather and weigh as much as a standard poodle or be encased in the most sophisticated electronic gadgetry. Organizational plans must be "strategic," which almost inevitably means that they are long, occupy many three-ring binders, and cost a great deal of money as a result of services delivered by exceptionally well-groomed strategic planning consultants. There is just one problem: there is no evidence that strategic planning, as it is often practiced, is related to organizational results. Kotter's devastating critique has been joined by others, including Schmoker (2004) and Fullan (2008). In fact, one recent study found an inverse relationship between the quality of the plan format and the results: the nicer and prettier the format, the worse the results (Reeves, 2006b). We are not saying that strategic planning is worthless, but rather we are saying that strategic planning practices can and must be improved. Some renewal coaches are also executive coaches who assist senior leaders with strategic plans. They are ideally equipped to help transform unwieldy and unworkable strategic plans into a more useful and productive method that links planning and execution. Simplicity and execution, not faux sophistication and elegance, are the essentials of effective plans.

The Results Myth

"I don't care how you do it," the manager barked, "just show me the results!" Scott Adams created the character Dilbert and we regularly enjoy his comic insight into the workplace. But one strip in particular troubled us, because it ridiculed "process pride." Surely the barking executive who cares only about results loved that one. Although we can all think of examples that justify the skepticism of process that Adams embraces, we should also hesitate to join the chorus that focuses exclusively on results.

First, results without purpose are not sustainable. Leaders are delusionary who think that people will celebrate a fundraising goal for a nonprofit without first being motivated by how those funds will be used for the people served by that organization. Corporate leaders are engaging in a fantasy when they think that goals such as market share, revenues, growth, or stock price will motivate people for the long term. The acid test question for sustainability is, If there were no money and no mandates, no reward and no punishments, no measurable return, would we still do this? If your visceral response is, Of course not—why would we do anything that was not associated with clear consequences? then let us suggest it has been too long since you considered the relationship of your plans to the greater good. Many people know right now that no matter how hard they work, they may not get a raise or bonus. They may not even keep their job. What could possibly encourage them to sustain their energy day after day? The only answer to this question is that they have a deep sense of purpose beyond the achievement of results (Bakke, 2005).

Second, a myopic focus on results is unhelpful in that it prevents you from achieving a deeper understanding of the causes of the results you seek. For example, if your goal is to lose weight, then drug abuse and eating disorders will frequently do the trick, but we don't recommend those strategies. In fact, we need a combination of insight into the causes of results and accurate measurement of the results themselves. Figure 16.2 illustrates the point. On the vertical axis is the achievement of results and on the horizontal axis is the understanding of causes—your work, task execution, cooperation, and engagement with others. As the lower left-hand quadrant illustrates, when there are low results and inadequate understanding of what caused poor results, we are in the unfortunate position of making the same mistake again and again. In this quadrant we find people who are losing—over and over again. In the book *Hard Facts, Dangerous Half-Truths, and Total Nonsense,* Pfeffer and Sutton (2006) provide examples from medicine, business, government, and education in which otherwise

Figure 16.2 The Results Myth

intelligent leaders are belligerently indifferent to the evidence before them and thus make the same errors year after year. In the upper left-hand quadrant, where there are high results but low understanding of the causes for those results, we find people who, at least temporarily, are *lucky*. Earnings have shot up and they look great on paper, but if the earnings improvement is associated with a short-term increase in the price of a commodity they sell or a short-term decrease in the cost of an operating division that was eliminated, then it is not at all clear that the earnings gain is sustainable. Commodity prices fluctuate, and people who think that a trend will always be followed appear to believe the myth that trees grow to the sky. Eliminating divisions may make sense, but too frequently what happens is that reductions in headcount have an adverse impact on service, quality, and reputation, which ultimately has an adverse impact on revenues and earnings. But the person focused only on results is indifferent to causes and long-term consequences.

In the lower right-hand quadrant are people and organizations with low results but a deep understanding of causes. For the results-driven leader, these "learners" are no different from the "losers" in the lower left-hand quadrant, because the results are similar. We would submit, however, that there is an exceptional degree of difference between the person with disappointing results who knows precisely why those results occurred and has a hundred-day plan to create improvements and the person with the same disappointing results who has no idea of or interest in the causes. The loser is doomed to repeat the mistakes, blaming every outside influence except his own failure to deepen his understanding. In the upper right-hand quadrant we find the leaders, those people and organizations with good results and a deep understanding of how they achieved them. They know not to rest on their laurels, however, because their ability to sustain good performance depends on a continued understanding of the processes and causes of their success.

The Control Myth

We all have two potential in-boxes on our desk. The first is a very large one that should be labeled "Things I cannot control." We know one executive, Kenneth, who has never acknowledged that such an in-box exists. When we examined his task list—a computerized list to which he had added everything he wanted to do to meet his growing commitments—it contained more than a thousand items. At first Kenneth insisted that there was really order amid the chaos, because many of his tasks had been carefully linked to the more than two hundred goals he had established for himself that year. He seemed to believe that the more things he committed to, the more he would get done. It became worse as Kenneth started maintaining not only his own task list but also a list for his direct reports. Then he started them for people who did not report to him. Although this frantic overcommitment in fact led inevitably to a loss of control over his time and daily activities, the endless lines of tasks created the illusion that he was in control. To reestablish a sense of sanity to his life, Kenneth did not need to prioritize the items on his list. He needed instead to challenge the entire premise of the list and that he was in control of as many things as he thought he was. We started with just one filter question: What could Kenneth personally control? That means that everything on the list that depended on someone else for action needed to be somewhere else. Perhaps it should be on that person's task list. Perhaps it should be on a collaborative project management board either in a conference room or in a shared web-based document system. In any case, if Kenneth did not control it, then it did not belong on his list. This filter alone shrunk the list to fewer than eighty items—certainly too long, but less than a tenth of the length of his original list.

DAILY DISCIPLINES IN ACTION

Renewal deserves your daily attention. More to the point, *you* deserve your daily attention. Everyone who depends on you financially and emotionally needs you to have renewal. The people who will benefit from your broadened focus on the greater good need you to have renewal. Your commitment to daily disciplines for renewal is not selfish but a commitment to empowering yourself for service. We know that not every daily discipline is healthy or appropriate. There are cases in which daily regimens are selfish and counterproductive; think of the person who goes to the gym three times a day to maintain a perfect body and then feeds his kids junk food and hits the bars most nights. The daily disciplines of renewal we advocate are not excessively time-consuming, but the first time you do them they will change your day, then your week, and over the course of time, your life.

The First Discipline: Values First, Tasks Second

You have a vision of who you are and who you want to become. You know what is important to you. Stephen Covey (1989) suggests that we write our own obituary to remind us of what we want people to say about us if we are suddenly gone from the scene. It is wise to reduce these ideas to a few words. Doug's late father, a law professor, bequeathed a small box full of index cards and small pieces of paper containing phrases that he thought were important, all recorded in his own hand. These phrases provide examples of how one might begin a day focused on values and purpose before proceeding to tasks. The first phrase addressed his general philosophy of life, and the second, his sense of his duties to his students. How might starting the day by focusing on only a few seconds of reflections change daily tasks?

> "All we need: love, justice, mercy, a sense of worth, a sense of place, a sense of belonging."
>
> "The vital process of the university is the one by which the student discovers who he is and what values he will choose to live by."

What are some words, phrases, or expressions that encapsulate your values?

____

____

The Second Discipline: Unify Every Demand for Your Time in a Single Place

Although it's easy to ridicule Kenneth's thousand-item task list, at least he had most of his tasks in one place. Worse than Kenneth are people who have the same thousand tasks, but some are inscribed in their planner, others written on Post-it notes and stuck to their computer screen, others entered into a computer task list, and still others recorded on their cell phone notes page. They spend more time thrashing about to find what they were supposed to do than they might have spent completing a task. Start the day with a single unified list. It does not matter if you use a FranklinCovey planner or blank sheets on a legal pad, as Mark McCormick (1984) did when he was operating one of the largest consulting firms in the world. Another chief executive we know uses index cards in his shirt pocket, a discipline that forces his daily list to be focused and brief. The first time you do this it may take a while, but after that it takes a very brief process of only a few minutes to create a single, unified list.

Describe how you will keep your list of daily activities and tasks. Identify exactly where it will be—in a planner or journal, on paper or the computer. Be specific so that you will know you have unified every demand for your time in a single place:

____

____

____

The Third Discipline: Set Boundaries on Technology

If audible warnings on your computer and cell phone alert you to incoming e-mail, turn them off right now. If you are expecting a call from a family member who is going into labor at any moment, then don't explain that to us in a meeting. Leave the meeting and go to be with your family member. Answer your priority incoming e-mail at specific times. For most busy executives, a three-time-per-day discipline will give your colleagues and customers excellent service and save you from wasting enormous amounts of time. For each e-mail there are only three things you can do. First, delete it before reading it. Even with excellent spam filters, many incoming e-mails belong in this category. Second, defer it. In most e-mail programs, such as Microsoft Outlook, e-mail can be quickly moved to a "pending" folder in a fraction of a second. Third, respond to it. When you rigidly adhere to the "delete, defer, or respond" rule, you will end every day with an empty e-mail box. Here's a challenge: Look at your e-mail inbox right now and count how many messages you have already read but have not yet acted on. It is not unusual for clients to tell us that there are hundreds of e-mails cluttering their inbox. No wonder they feel overwhelmed.

Another boundary you can set on technology is an organizational one. No matter how hard we plead with people to stop using the reply-all function, which leads to incalculable wasted time for many unnecessary recipients, people still do it. The simple solution is to use a "rule," allowed by most e-mail programs, that will screen out anything that was sent to you as a "copy" rather than as an original recipient. We know one senior executive with global responsibilities for more than ten thousand people who did this his first day on the job after noticing the preponderance of "cc" messages he received. When he took himself out of the endless reply loop, people soon got the message that he would consider only mail directed to him, and if it was directed to him, it needed to be important enough to require a decision.

Many of us enjoy e-mail lists, blogs, RSS feeds, and so on. But these too can be quickly overwhelming and divert attention from your primary focus. The technology boundary here is the creation of a separate e-mail identity. You can probably unsubscribe to most of the e-mail lists you are now on without any deep sense of loss. But for those lists you would still like to be on (the daily cartoon from the *New Yorker* is one of our favorites) disassociate them from your regular e-mail identity and create a new identity with one of the many free providers. You can then make a decision to look at those e-mail boxes when they become a priority for you. To remind yourself of the purpose of this e-mail address, you can register a creative user names, such as TimeWaster@aol.com or GetBackToWork@gmail.com or ICannotBelieveIamDoingThis@yahoo.com.

Identify the technology boundaries you can set immediately:

____

____

____

Identify the technology boundaries you can set in the next hundred days:

____

____

____

The Fourth Discipline: Scheduled Time for Peace and Focus

If you leave your home or place of work to attend a meeting and someone calls, what is the caller told? "I'm sorry, Jane is not available now, she's in a meeting." According to our observations, most meetings are not terribly important, yet out of duty and habit you attend. What if you were engaged in work on an important project at home or in the office and the phone rang? Almost never does it feel legitimate to respond, "I'm sorry, I'm working on a project." The inevitable rejoinder is, "This will just take a minute," and whether it is one minute or sixty, the interruption trumps your project almost every time. Therefore, we have learned, you must schedule time for peace, quiet, and focusing with the same priority and same boundaries as a meeting. In today's environment, closing the door or not answering the phone simply does not work. You have to schedule the time in such a way that it is clear you are not available. Just two of these "meetings" for ninety minutes, twice a week, would provide three hours of absolutely uninterrupted time. When was the last time you had three hours of uninterrupted time? In the unlikely event that you can recall such a period, we are willing to bet that it was at night or on a weekend. The culture of collaboration, ordinarily a fine thing, has rendered focus and peace as illegitimate pursuits during the work day. The culture does, however, allow you to go to a meeting, and we therefore suggest that you perhaps schedule a couple of your "meetings" in a library, conference room, or office designated for visitors. The key is that you have ninety minutes in which you are unavailable for interruptions and invisible to those who, however well-meaning, would seek to break your concentration and deny you the peace and focus you need.

Identify the time, date, and location of your next meeting for peace and focus:

____

____

____

The Fifth Discipline: The Do-Not-Do List

We have argued elsewhere that you must "pull the weeds before you plant the flowers" (Reeves, 2006b). The truth is, you already have a do-not-do list, but it was almost certainly created by default. We decide what not to do when we are exhausted and out of energy and have lost our concentration. Sometimes the things on the default do-not-do list are trivial; other times they are vital but we have simply lost sight of them amid the chaos of life. If you wish to create a do-not-do list by design rather than by default, you might start by showing your present task list to a coach or colleague. If you are fortunate enough to have an assistant or colleague in whom you can confide, show them your present list. Every time, bar none, we have had clients do this exercise, the assistant or colleague reviewing the list does not take offense or assume that the executive is trying to avoid work. Rather, their uniform question is, "Why in the world is this on your list?" This question is typically followed by some very practical insights, including, "That's my job, please let me do it" or "I already did it; you don't need to worry about that" or "You are three days behind on an incredibly important project and it's starting to affect other departments, so let me help shift some of these items around."

List just five things that you can place on your do-not-do list right now:

____

____

____

____

____

The Sixth Discipline: Pause for the Greater Good

Some of the most effective and busy people we know find regular renewal by way of a disciplined commitment to the greater good. Although some of them have done extraordinary work—such as building schools and hospitals around the world—most of them have a more incremental approach: a commitment to small acts of service on a frequent basis. One person we know pauses for the greater good by going to the parking lot after a snowstorm and anonymously cleaning the windshields of the cars of colleagues and strangers. No one knows he does this. Another serves at a homeless shelter on several holidays each year to give the regular staff a break. Another leads a weekly study group for struggling adult readers. These are small acts, requiring only a few minutes. None of these people said that their commitment to the greater good would occur "when I have the time," because they knew that they would always be busy in their professional and personal lives, both now and into retirement.

Think of something you can do in the next seven days that will renew your spirit in pursuit of the greater good. Think small—a single act of kindness, helping an organization, or doing something extra for a cause you already support. Don't make it an extra burden; think of something you already do during the day to give yourself a "renewal break" that will also help someone else:

____

____

____

____

____

The Seventh Discipline: Renewing Others

You have already learned the value of each element of the Renewal Coaching framework, and you have already learned the value of rigorous self-assessment and deep insight. How can you help at least one colleague, friend, or family member gain a similar insight? You don't need to give them a book or send them to a Web site. You could just share with them something you have learned. If you saw a great movie or sporting event last weekend, you would not hesitate to bring that up in a casual discussion. In addition to the banter about "That was a great performance!" or "What a lousy play by the shortstop!" perhaps you could add, "I learned something really interesting yesterday."

You renew others most of all with your actions, not your words. When you take time for physical renewal, you show your colleagues that even busy and effective people can take time for a walk or a run, that effective marketing dinners don't have to include alcohol, and that the healthy food in the cafeteria is not just for those with perfect bodies. When you take time for emotional renewal, you show your loved ones that you are not taking them for granted. Your unexpected and unsolicited acts of appreciation to a colleague show them that you appreciate them for who they are as a person, not just for their labor. If there are people in your life with whom there is emotional strain, there will never be a better time than today to begin the healing process with a card or a call. Even long-term and deep emotional divisions can be healed, and the one who takes the risk and initiates the healing will experience emotional renewal whether or not the division is mended. When you take time for spiritual renewal, you need not proselytize anyone. Rather, you heed the words of St. Francis: Preach the gospel at all times; when necessary, use words. In a pluralistic world there are many gospels and many spiritual paths. Whether you surrender to the beauty of a stunning sunset or a magnificent building, a glorious moon, or an incredible piece of music, you make way for inspiration and awe in a world dominated by rationality. When you allow yourself to slip into these worlds of wonder, you are giving those around you the signal that even the most analytical among us find renewal not only in our minds but in our spirits.

Think of at least one way that you can renew others today:

____

____

WHEN YOU ARE STUCK

Getting stuck is not a possibility, but a certainty. There will be days that evaporate, plans that implode, and people who aggravate you beyond belief. Renewal will, at those times, sound like a pipe dream. "One more hot idea down the drain," intones your most critical inner voice. Be prepared for this and have a tool kit ready to help you get refocused and reenergized.

First, keep your hundred-day plan with you. We carry our plans—just a few pages—with us in our travels around the world. Whenever things start to get crazy, we can stop and get refocused on what we know, because the current span of one hundred days is most important.

Second, connect to the Renewal Coaching community. At www.RenewalCoaching.com you can click on Getting Unstuck and find stories of people who have been through the same challenges as you, and get personal assistance from others.

Third, find a touchstone—something or someone that keeps you grounded. For some people it's a spouse, for others a pet, for others a specific piece of music or work of art. When Doug hears the Bach Prelude and Fugue in C Major, it creates three minutes of tranquility and beauty. When Olé, Elle's Vizla, falls asleep in her arms, the most traumatic events of the day take a backseat to the snoring of this wonderful dog.

You are not alone on this journey, and you will find support in places and things that will take on new levels of meaning every time you look at them through the lens of renewal.

CHAPTER 17

Measuring Your Success

Effective application of the Renewal Coaching framework creates results for both the individual and the organization. These results include visible changes in the following areas:

- Personal well-being through activities that ensure renewal for the individual and lead to satisfaction on a daily basis
- Organizational well-being and comfort through renewal of relationships, collaboration, and conflict resolution
- Personal well-being sustained by renewal that brings efficiency to the work the person does
- Organizational well-being through the effective accomplishment of goals and the implementation of strategies that ensure financial success and growth
- Sustained change through renewal activities directed toward a focus on the greater good

Individuals and organizations can and should monitor the progress of their Renewal Project by identifying the indicators that let them know if they are moving in the right direction. Both profit and nonprofit organizations typically have quarterly and annual measures in place. Individuals don't always think in terms of this structure, but more frequent reviews are far more likely to sustain effective change than an annual (and depressing) review of half-hearted resolutions penned the previous January. For example, a person who wants to increase personal renewal habits could count the number of occasions of interpersonal renewal and evaluate the quality of those experiences. This sort of frequent and specific feedback helps sustain worthwhile activities.

Outside of the typical business structure are opportunities to celebrate short-term wins. Short-term wins help people find energy through recognition, feedback, and celebration. When these wins are directly related to the greater good, they are vital sources of renewal.

What Do You Already Know?

Before you continue, use the space below to gather your thoughts about what you already know about the nature and purpose of short-term wins. Give some examples of how you have used short-term wins in other projects or in other areas of your life:

____

____

____

____

____

____

____

____

SHORT-TERM WINS

Consider the scenario of Davis, the manager of the financial institution introduced in Chapter Thirteen, who found meaning in his work and life when he thought about leveraging the company's work for the good of new businesses trying to establish themselves and thrive during tough economic times. Here are some of the short-term wins Davis anticipated and therefore checked into on a regular basis:

- The percentage of employees whose experience with a pro-bono client gave them credibility to work with a paying client
- The percentage of pro-bono clients who report an increase in the accomplishment of specific actions in their work within two weeks after a session with a consultant
- The development dollars saved each month because of on-the-job experiences provided through the pro-bono program
- The number of senior consultants who participate in the pro-bono program (indicating the depth of support for this initiative)
- The number of employees who report having accepted the job at Davis's company over others, because they were drawn by the pro-bono program
- The percentage of paying clients who report they want to hire this company because they admire the work being done by the pro-bono program
- The number of times the company pro-bono program is mentioned or featured in media about the community
- The percentage of people and professionals in other industries who know about the pro-bono program and wish to emulate it

You get the idea. Davis may not begin by formally measuring all of these indicators, but by thinking them through in advance, he and the other people in the company are more likely to notice them, ask about them, measure them, and broadcast them. The beautiful thing about thinking this way is that more and more people involved get in the habit of looking for short-term wins and know the importance of communicating them and celebrating them every chance they get.

Davis could make each of these short-term wins even more specific and informative if he analyzed them within significant subgroups related to the greater good. For example, he could look at each short-term win relative to women, minority groups, and people starting second careers. He could also analyze the regions or neighborhoods within the area served by his company or industry.

Before you dismiss the idea of pro-bono work—that is, offering services without cost—let us consider both sides of the argument on these sensitive subjects. Both prevailing extremes are, we believe, wrong. At one end of the continuum are those who say, "I know what I'm worth, and if people don't want to pay it, then they can simply do without my services." At the other extreme are those who believe, "I'm not really worth what I'm charging, and therefore I'll offer a discount to anyone who asks—nonprofits, government, corporations down on their luck—I'm just lucky to have an engagement." We believe that the middle ground is preserved by the "better free than cheap" rule. If you discount your services for one client, word will soon spread that you are not as valuable as you claim to be. Only fools pay retail, or so the reasoning goes. But if you provide your services only to the highest bidder, you may gain the world and lose your soul, as St. Paul and common sense have both warned. The middle ground, we believe, is in the "better free than cheap" rule. That is, if you are offering services that, for the sake of argument, are worth $7,500 per day and the client cannot pay it, then rather than discount your services and thereby depress your income from all clients forever, consider offering your services for *free.* That's right: you don't counter an offer of $3,000 to your offer of $7,000 with something "in the middle," such as $5,000. Rather, you say, "If you can't pay my fee, I understand, and because I value a long-term future relationship with you, I will do this engagement without a single penny of cost to you. If you offer an honorarium that is lower than my usual fee, please make out a check to a charity of your choice."

This is a startling proposition for many clients, but it is the right position to take. In some religious traditions, giving away 10 percent of your income or, in the case of people whose time is money, 10 percent of your time, is an obligation. Therefore, if you are planning on a hundred engagements this year, consider giving away ten of them. When someone complains about your fees, you can say in good conscience, "I understand, and I've accommodated that through my policy of giving away ten free days each year. I've done this for the local hospital, as well as for the Zen Center and the Sisters of Charity. I still have two free days left this year, and I'm happy to include you on the list. When would it be convenient for me to speak to your group?"

Whether the client accepts your kind offer or defers, reluctant to be cast in the same boat as the other recipients of your largess, you have made your company a force in the consulting field. You have also refused to bargain on price, a critical policy for people who offer valuable services in exchange for a promise to be paid.

Where Are Your Short-Term Wins?

What are the obvious short-term wins for the project you identified to ultimately contribute to a greater good? List at least ten ideas here. Be sure to express them as an indicator (a statistic of some sort, such as percentage, dollars, number) so you can measure them:

Now think of ten more short-term wins that are less rational, less obvious. Rather than numbers, think of the great feeling you had when you gave a friendly greeting to someone in the lobby, or think of the look on the face of the soldier in the airport for whom you anonymously bought lunch.

One last time: How can you analyze the indicators you wrote for your short-term wins so that you have even more specific information that can teach the company what works?

____

____

____

____

____

CAPTURE THE LEARNING

The data about short-term wins are only as good as what individuals and organizations learn from them. To do this, you must reflect on the actions that preceded, catalyzed, or led up to the short-term win. These actions may be specific to the strategies that have been selected and are being implemented to move the project forward, or they may be actions taken somewhere else in the system that were not deliberate but coincidentally are causing a desirable effect.

For example, we knew a teacher who noticed that certain students who had previously engaged in a significant amount of misbehavior in class were more frequently doing what they were supposed to do. This was a highly desirable win, to say the least, but she did not know why it was happening. She made a list of the changes she could think of that might be related. When she asked her colleagues what they thought, she learned that the support teacher had modified her time from helping kids learn content after they had already failed in the classroom to helping students learn the content for the next day's class. The impact was that the students were less frustrated in class because they were already beginning to understand what they needed to learn, so they did not misbehave as often. The faculty talked about this astounding effect, scaled up the approach for several weeks, and found that it had a similar impact on other students. Within two months they had changed the entire school schedule and program and made the new model their practice and policy.

What learning cycle will you put in place to "mine" the data for all the insights they have to offer? How will you examine the causes of your results?

____

____

____

____

____

BACK TO YOUR 100-DAY RENEWAL PROJECT

Review your 100-Day Renewal Project and revise your plan on the basis of the insights you obtained from the exercises in this chapter. What specific actions will you take in the next hundred days to identify short-term wins, communicate them to others, and celebrate them with everyone who cares? Once again, use the LEAD technique:

What do you need to LEARN?

What EVIDENCE do you need to collect and analyze?

What ATTITUDES and expectations must be developed?

What DECISIONS must be made?

CHAPTER 18

Giving Back

Christina Baldwin (2005) is a storycatcher. She devotes her life's work to helping people and organizations use their stories to learn about themselves and one another. Christina's work proves that when we listen to one another's stories, we perceive the meaning in events and recognize these events as powerful learning moments. As a renewal coach or as an individual or leader in an organization using the Renewal Coaching process and perspective, you have stories to tell and stories to hear. Through the international Renewal Coaching community and network, you have a place to post your own story or to tell us the story of someone you coach. We also welcome the stories of renewal coaches and what it was like for them to coach someone through the Renewal Coaching process. Log onto www.RenewalCoaching.com and let us hear from you!

Ten Great Reasons to Tell Your Story

1. To inspire other people and organizations.
2. To make visible and empower those who are the most vulnerable in our society by giving them a face and a name.
3. To be a leader reaching for the pinnacle of your passion. All people who aspire to lead, no matter what their field, passion, or skills—whether they are artists, scientists, athletes, thinkers, inventors, or dreamers—all find a way to tell their story to a global audience.

4. To celebrate publicly your success and the success of everyone involved.
5. To strengthen your networks of support. You do not know what will happen, but you do know that when you tell your story, someone else in the world will respond, often from surprising quarters.
6. To challenge yourself to know what you did in your journey toward renewal—the actions you took and the effect they had (connecting cause and effect).
7. To attract key allies to your passion, widen your circle of influence, and make an even bigger difference for the greater good.
8. To widen your circle of influence on others. To put yourself "out there" so you can be found and contacted by those who want to follow in your footsteps and who need a mentor.
9. To receive with humility the gratitude of others so that you can continue to give.
10. To teach and learn.

Your Renewal Story

You have a renewal story worth telling! Here are some questions to think through as you craft the story you have to tell. Use the spaces provided to record what you know so far. Return to this section often to add significant information.

How did it all begin? Many renewal projects begin because of a specific challenge, adversity, or loss. Is this true for you or your organization? Tell the beginning of your story here:

What is the greater good? To whom does this matter?

What is the title of your renewal project and what is the work? Describe here your strategies and significant actions:

(continued)

Your Renewal Story (continued)

Why does this matter to the people doing the work?

____

____

____

Who are the significant people involved?

____

____

What is most innovative about this work?

____

____

What have been the key turning points and breakthroughs?

____

____

____

What is the impact of this work on people, families, the community, the region, and the world?

____

____

____

What is next?

____

____

____

PARTING THOUGHTS

Please do not limit the sharing of your stories to the Renewal Coaching community and network. Tell your story in your professional organizations, alumni groups and religious affiliations, in family gatherings, at happy hour with friends, and while engaging in your hobbies. You can blog about it, and use other social networking sites such as Twitter, Facebook, LinkedIn, and YouTube. Leaders of organizations have additional communication resources for telling their story of renewal. Seek opportunities to make presentations within your organization and to civic and community groups; contribute your stories to newsletters and professional journals; and post them on your Web site.

Finally, we remind you that your life is already meaningful. We are here to support you in your renewal journey so you can live it mindfully and make a difference for others.

REFERENCES

AA Services. (2001). *Alcoholics anonymous* (4th ed.). New York: Alcoholics Anonymous World Services.

Allen, D. (2001). *Getting things done: The arts of stress-free productivity*. New York: Penguin Putnam.

Bakke, D. W. (2005). *Joy at work: A revolutionary approach to fun on the job*. Seattle: PVG.

Baldwin, C. (2005). *Storycatcher: Making sense of our lives through the power and practice of story*. Novato, CA: New World Library.

Bossidy, L., & Charan, R. (2002). *Execution: The discipline of getting things done*. New York: Crown Business.

Boyatzis, R. E., & McKee, A. (2005). *Resonant leadership: Renewing yourself and connecting with others through mindfulness, hope, and compassion*. Boston: Harvard Business School Press.

Casciaro, T., & Lobo, M. S. (2005, June 1). Competent jerks, lovable fools, and the formation of social networks. *Harvard Business Review*, *83*(6), 92–99.

Collins, J. (2001). *Good to great: Why some companies make the leap . . . and others don't*. New York: HarperCollins.

Coutu, D., & Kauffman, C. (2009). What coaches can do for you. *Harvard Business Review*, *87*(1), 91–92.

Covey, S. R. (1989). *The seven habits of highly effective people: Powerful lessons in personal change*. New York: Fireside Books.

Crenshaw, D. (2008). *The myth of multitasking: How "doing it all" gets nothing done*. San Francisco: Jossey-Bass.

Cummings, G. T., & Worley, C. G. (2005). *Organization development and change* (8th ed.). Mason, OH: South-Western Publishing.

Daly, P. H., & Watkins, M. (2006). *The first ninety days in government: Critical success strategies for new public managers at all levels*. Boston: Harvard Business School Press.

Dweck, C. S. (2006). *Mindset: The new psychology of success*. New York: Random House.

Encarta World English Dictionary (2009). New York: St. Martin's Press. http://encarta.msn.com/encnet/features/dictionary/dictionaryhome.aspx

Fullan, M. (2008). *The six secrets of change: What the best leaders do to help their organizations survive and thrive*. San Francisco: Jossey-Bass.

Goleman, D. (Ed.) (2003). *Healing emotions: Conversations with the Dalai Lama on mindfulness, emotions, and health.* Boston: Shambala.

Goleman, D., Boyatzis, R., & McKee, A. (2002). *Primal leadership: Realizing the power of emotional intelligence.* Boston: Harvard Business School Press.

Hannon, K. (2009, October 8). Boomers redefine retirement with 'Encore' careers. In US News & World Report. Retrieved October 14, 2009, from http://www.usnews.com/money/personal-finance/articles/2009/10/08/boomers-redefine-retirement-with-encore-careers.html.

Howe, N., & Strauss, W. (2000). *Millennials rising: The next great generation.* New York: Vintage Books.

Kotter, J. P. (2006). *Leading change.* Boston: Harvard Business School Press.

Kotter, J. P. (2007, January). Leading change: Why transformation efforts fail. *Harvard Business Review, 85*(1), 96–103.

Lynch, J. (2000). *A cry unheard: New insights into the medical consequences of loneliness.* Baltimore: Bancroft Press.

McCormick, M. H. (1984). *What they don't teach you at Harvard Business School: Notes from a street-smart executive.* New York: Bantam Books.

Merriam, S. B., & Caffarella, R. S. (1999). *Learning in adulthood: A comprehensive guide* (2nd ed.). San Francisco: Jossey-Bass.

Nance-Nash, Sheryl (2009, January/February). The 100-day turnaround. *Arrive,* 32–35.

Pfeffer, J., & Sutton, R. I. (2000). *The knowing-doing gap: How smart companies turn knowledge into action.* Boston: Harvard Business School Press.

Pfeffer, J., & Sutton, R. I. (2006). *Hard facts, dangerous half-truths, and total nonsense: Profiting from evidence-based management.* Boston: Harvard Business School Press.

Rameau, J-P. (1722; 1971). *Treatise on harmony* (Philip Gossett, Trans.). Mineola, NY: Dover Publications.

Random House dictionary of the English language (2nd ed.). (1987). New York: Random House.

Reeves, D. B. (2006a). *The learning leader: How to focus school improvement for better results.* Alexandria, VA: Association for Supervision and Curriculum Development.

Reeves, D. B. (2006b, September). Pull the weeds before you plant the flowers. *Educational Leadership, 64*(1), 89–90.

Reeves, D. B. (2008). *Reframing leadership to improve your school.* Alexandria, VA: Association for Supervision and Curriculum Development.

Reeves, D. B., & Allison, E. (2009). *Renewal coaching: Sustainable change for individuals and organizations.* San Francisco: Jossey-Bass.

Savitz, A. W., & Weber, K. (2006). *The triple bottom line: How today's best-run companies are achieving economic, social, and environmental success—and how you can too.* San Francisco: Jossey-Bass.

Schmoker, M. J. (2004). Tipping point: From feckless reform to substantive instructional improvement. *Phi Delta Kappan, 85*(6), 424–432.

Scoular, P. A. (2009). What coaches can do for you. *Harvard Business Review, 87*(1), 96.

Shoshanna, B. (2003). *Zen and the art of falling in love.* New York: Simon & Schuster.

Sternberg, R. J. (Ed.) (2000). *Handbook of intelligence.* Cambridge, UK: Cambridge University Press.

Sutton, R. I. (2007). *The no asshole rule: Building a civilized workplace and surviving one that isn't.* New York: Business Plus.

Weisbord, M. R. (1987). *Productive workplaces: Organizing and managing for dignity, meaning, and community.* San Francisco: Jossey-Bass.

Wheatley, M., & Chodron, P. (1999, November). It starts with uncertainty. *Shambala Sun.* Retrieved January 15, 2009, from http://www.margaretwheatley.com/articles/uncertainty.html

INDEX

Index